t'ai chi

37 steps to happiness

37 steps to happiness

t'ai chi

WITH AN INTRODUCTION TO
AQUA T'AI-CHI

PETER CHIN KEAN CHOY

THE LYONS PRESS
Guilford, Connecticut
An imprint of The Globe Pequot Press

First Lyons Press edition, 2001

The Lyons Press is an imprint of The Globe Pequot Press.

Originally published in Great Britain by Kyle Cathie Limited, 2001

Edited by Caroline Taggart
Photography by Chris Cormack
Designed by Ted Kinsey
Production by Lorraine Baird and Sha Huxtable

Picture credits:

Still pictures: pages 2 (Dominique Delfino), 21 (Werner H Muller), 67 (Patrice Labarbe), 149 (Alex S. MacLean) and 179 (Frederic Denhez); Science Photo Library: pages 85 (John Mead), and 99 (Mehau Kulyk); NHPA page 159 (R. Sorensen & J. Olsen).

The illustrations on pages 19, 165 and 189 are by the author.

Printed and bound in Singapore by Kyodo Printing Co.

ISBN 1-58574-415-8

The Library of Congress Cataloging-in-Publication Data is available on file.

A note on the dragon illustration: In ancient times, in China, the dragon symbolized wisdom, health and prosperity. The symbol of the three dragons in this book (pages 21, 67, 85 and 99) connotes the balance of the Yin (feminine/mother), Yang (masculine/father) and Tao (creative/child) principles. The dragons guide the reader On the Plains —The Calling to Return Home; To the Mountain—The Journey to Find the True Self; joining Heaven, Humanity and Earth—Finding the Circle of Life; and sharing Happiness in Service—Fulfillment.

CONTENTS

Acknowledgements

Most of all, I wish to thank my father, Chin Ket Leong, and my mother, Yong Liu Keow, who have both now passed away. Although they did not live to see this book, their spirit of courage, devotion and wisdom flows through these pages.

I also want to thank my grandfather, Yong Mun Sen, who was a true Father of Malaysian Painting. He was, in the 1940s, already sharing with those around him, and through his work, the urgent need to build bridges between Eastern and Western artistic expression. He inspired me to keep the flame glowing and strong for future generations.

I have so many wonderful T'ai-Chi and Chi Kung teachers to thank, many of whom are mentioned in my Preface. I wish them many more years of good health and happy service.

I also dedicate this book to so many relatives and friends who helped me along my path when I was just a young lad – my brothers Edward, Tommy, Philip and David, and sisters Helen and Elizabeth.

To my dearest Tao, Gael, Melchi and Triune, thank you, you have always been an inspiration to me and, whether you were near or far, you have always been in my heart.

A big thank you to some dear friends who have deeply touched me with their unique wonderful presences – Myriam, Francine, Chan, Yap, Wan, David Slorpe, Jan Slorpe, Angeles de Luque, Low Beng Imm, Herman, Wing Hon, Ranjit Kaur, Cornelius Bong, Surinder Singh, Tan Lay Peng and all my school friends.

I am also deeply indebted to all my Foundation T'ai-Chi Chi Kung and T'ai-Chi Form students, who have been so inspirational. You came from all over the world and helped me create the Rainbow T'ai-Chi School. It is your special talents, energies and questions that have helped to shape Rainbow T'ai-Chi into not only a Health and Rejuvenation system of exercises but also a way of life.

Last but not least, I want to thank my publishers Kyle Cathie and the team (especially Caroline Taggart), Ted Kinsey the designer, Christopher Cormack the photographer, Catherine Blake the copy-editor and everybody behind the scene who held my 'Big Baby Book Project' together! It is thanks to your trust in my ability that I wanted to give even more of my energies to it, and to make this dream come true. The baby is here!!

I want to send my appreciation to all the radiant, wise, Nature presences I have come to meet and was often moved to tears feeling their loving and electrifying energy pouring through me from them, especially under the waterfalls of Ulu Kanching, Malaysia; at the Trinity College on Mount Sophia, Singapore; under the Bodhi Tree, India; on the bay at the Findhorn Foundations, Scotland; at Harbin Hotsprings and Stewart Mineral Springs near Mount Shasta, California; at the T'ai-Chi Farm in New York, America; on the Hautes Alpes of Southern France; on the Hua Shan Taoist Mountains in China; on top of Mount Sinai and swimming with the Dolphin from the Red Sea in Egypt; dancing in Tintagel Valley of Cornwall... infinite thanks go to 'you all', with all my heart, body, mind and spirit. Thank you for showing me that the Rainbow T'ai-Chi Dimensions really do exist in Nature.

Preface

Ever since the publication of my first book, *T'ai-Chi Chi Kung: 15 Ways to a Happier You*, in June 1998, I have received letters from all over the world, thanking me for writing it. So, to the thousands of people who let me know how valuable the book has proved to them personally, thank you, too. I hope you will find this book even more enriching.

In the first volume, I focused on the ways in which you can achieve a 'happier you' using fifteen basic T'ai-Chi exercises and principles. This book builds from that in the same way that the notes on a piano can be combined in forms and patterns to create a beautiful piece of music. The thirty-seven steps set out here are mirrors that will show you who you truly are: a radiant, harmonious being of pure energy ('chi'). The pathways ('chi meridians') of energy in your body flow like rivers of sparkling energy from your limbs into your tan-tien, or belly centre (the sea of energy) and then spread out through the internal organs and the spine and upper limbs. In my first book I concentrated on the river of chi; this book connects that river to the sea of ecstatic chi in your heart, body, mind and spirit.

Another exciting event in the summer of 1998 was the inauguration of the Rainbow T'ai-Chi School, a long-cherished dream of mine that became reality thanks to the immense generosity of one of my students. The school is a 5-acre property situated in a beautiful part of Devon, 15 minutes from Dartmoor to the west, with the highest waterfalls in England, and 15 minutes from the sea to the east. The inauguration took place in the same week that *15 Ways to a Happier You* was published!

Inauguration of the school, June 1998

Even though the school is still so new, we have already begun many initiatives that welcome and train new students. These embody principles and practices that can be easily adopted at home. Each student who comes here brings a little tree to plant in the grounds, and practises by the tree. I recommend practising with a growing tree, or a houseplant if you do not have a garden; it helps you to understand the Tao as the way of Nature, and to root and develop your personal self-confidence.

Many experienced students spend time doing 'chi service' – allowing cosmic chi to flow into whatever they do. This is something else that I would encourage all T'ai-Chi students to explore once they are sufficiently experienced. At the school, where 'chi service' is at its most concentrated, many visitors and participants have remarked on the harmonious atmosphere they can feel, and tell me how it has helped them recover their sense of inner joy.

Participants in my summer school practising the Rainbow Aqua T'ai-Chi Form in the school pool, 2000.

In 1999, my dream of having an Aqua T'ai-Chi swimming pool was also realized, and this was where we held our New Millennium Celebration. Many people throughout the world believe that this new millennium is the Age of Aquarius, when people will learn to flow, in peace and harmony, and with loving energy. There can be no better way to learn how do to this than to practise this ancient art of T'ai-Chi in water!

Normally, people take many years to grasp the T'ai-Chi principles of fluidity, but by practising in a pool, you can learn it in a few weeks. Water possesses special healing qualities, which you will learn about later in this book, and these complement the naturally beneficial movements of the exercises. Students have told me of a cathartic feeling of emotional release, relief from tension with the river, sea and land. Your rewards are the pots of golden, happy chi energy at the beginning and end of your Rainbow Aqua T'ai-Chi practice!

Meeting the masters

Many students of T'ai-Chi complain that books on the subject generally do not give much background information about the T'ai-Chi teachers unless they are dead, in which case all the information on them has to be written by others. This is true in so many areas of life. My grandfather, Yong Mun Sen, was an artist. He loved painting and worked very hard. In the 1940s he became the first Malaysian to exhibit his paintings in England, Australia and America, and in 1953, his paintings were shown alongside works by Degas, Matisse and Picasso. But it was only after his death in 1962 that he was

Taoist Grandmaster Abbot Liu Xing and myself at Hua Shan Mountain Temple.

and pain, and many other incredible healing sensations they have experienced while in water.

Although the emphasis of Aqua T'ai-Chi falls mainly on fluidity, it also functions as an introduction to the Rainbow T'ai-Chi Form. When you learn Aqua T'ai-Chi, it feels as if you are becoming the misty rainwater droplets in the sky and the rivers. When you learn Rainbow T'ai-Chi Form, it feels as if you are becoming the rainbow that links the sky

With Grandmaster Chen, his wife and grandchild at Chen Village, China.

proclaimed by the Malaysian press 'the Father of Malaysian Painting', and today his works are sought after by the major art auction houses of the world.

In my late teens, I found myself experiencing the art of T'ai-Chi as a beautiful unfolding process of self-discovery. There was this fresh, unknown quality about it that went beyond its function as physical exercise for fitness and relaxation. At the end of a session, I sometimes had to ask myself: 'Did I just do that?' Some people were moved to tears when they saw how beautiful the movements were. Of course, I did not have the intention of creating such an impact. Although I was learning in the same hall as many of my T'ai-Chi teachers and fellow students, I often felt as if I was being transported into different dimensions. At one class, for example, it seemed as though I was being bathed in pure light, and tingling with chi energy all over. My fellow students experienced nothing of this. When I pursued this further with more experienced T'ai-Chi and Chi Kung healing teachers in China and meditation teachers in India, I discovered that I had been experiencing chi energy, and that I should treasure these experiences always.

I was in China recently, making my final preparations for this book. I visited the T'ai-Chi and Taoist monks at Hua Shan ('Flower') Mountain, where for thousands of years the Taoists have reverently pursued the promotion of health and rejuvenation. After climbing about 1,600 feet up this glorious mountain, the rain fell briefly, and then suddenly a rainbow emerged, followed by another rainbow underneath it, to connect the highest peaks with the valleys and rivers. I felt exhilarated.

My father, who was a Chinese medical doctor and Martial Arts master, had a life-long wish, which was to visit and pay his respects to the ancient Taoist masters in China. Unfortunately he passed away before he achieved his ambition. I shared this message with the masters everywhere I went, and did it on his behalf. I believe his spirit is well pleased.

I met the Taoist Grandmaster Liu Xing Yi, who is Abbot of the Yu Quan Yuan ('Jade Spirit') Temple, one of the largest Taoist temples in China; we talked about our common purposes, and he felt inspired when he heard of

Wudang Tai-Chi Master Wu with me outside a Taoist temple in the foothills of Hua Shan mountain, China.

the principles and activities we are putting into practise. In America I also met and studied with Professor Jou Tsung Hwa, scholar, T'ai-Chi teacher and author of many T'ai-Chi and Taoist books. He talked to me about the ancient T'ai-Chi masters, and told me: 'Master Chang San Feng transformed T'ai-Chi Chuan from a martial technique into a way of improving the heart, body, mind and spirit, thus enabling one to progress through the stage of tranquillity ultimately to enter the world of the fourth dimension. T'ai-Chi embodies a philosophy that not only promotes health but can also be applied to every aspect of our daily life.' It is on this ancient theme that this book is based.

The First Master

It is generally believed that Chang San Feng (1279–1368), a Taoist priest, was the founder of T'ai-Chi Chuan. He was influenced by Taoism, initially a pure nature philosophy of chi and balance, whose origins could be traced as far back as 1122 BC when the I Ching ('Book of Changes') was introduced. When the Han Dynasty came to power in 206 BC, Taoist philosophy fell under the influence of Buddhism and Confucianism, and was translated into a religious context. The theories of Buddhism were about reaching enlightenment, or buddhahood, whereas Confucianism was concerned with a complex set of values governing human behaviour. Martial Arts groups then translated the Taoist philosophy into a system of fighting, especially from the Liang Dynasty (AD 502-557) onwards. At the same time, the Pure Nature Taoists such as Lao Tze, together with Taoist medical scholars, focused on aspects of health and rejuvenation for the development of human life.

It was for this purpose that Master Chang founded a Taoist temple in Wudang Mountain. He taught mental, emotional and physical exercises based on the harmony of Yin/Yang/Tao principles, as a way to improve people's health. At that time, hard Martial Arts systems, such as the Shaolin, were focusing on rigorous physical and spiritual training and were known as 'Wai Dan' ('External Elixir'). T'ai-Chi Chuan was known as 'Nei Dan' ('Internal Elixir'). Master Chang was also respected as an advisor on Taoist philosophy at the highest level. It was in this way that T'ai-Chi came to be regarded originally as the 'Ultimate Art of Life', and T'ai-Chi masters were revered as Masters of Wisdom who were authorities on every aspect of daily life, including education, medicine, justice and agriculture.

According to information passed down through many generations of teachers, Master Chang learned T'ai-Chi in

I am certified to teach Zhineng Chi Kung by Dr Pang Ming.

a dream, and it was later confirmed to him by his observations of nature. He saw a crane and a snake engaged in a fight that looked more like a dance. He noticed how the snake would recoil to avoid the crane's aggression and use that same recoil to launch its own attack. The crane would use its wings to cover the snake softly. He recognized Yin (the yielding principle) as nature's way of dealing with Yang (the assertive principle). This, in the context of human interaction, was about learning to be humble, pliable and soft in order to deal with aggressive, hurtful and hard attitudes. This balanced understanding of Yin/receptive and Yang/assertive principles was applied in the sphere of the healing arts, and helped to transform illness into an opportunity to accumulate more chi for health and rejuvenation.

The History of T'ai-Chi Chuan

Throughout Chinese history, periods of unrest encouraged reactive attitudes. Even T'ai-Chi practitioners were involved in the enforcement of law and order, and instruction in the Martial Arts aspect of T'ai-Chi was over-emphasized while the philosophical and meditative aspects were gradually forgotten.

In more peaceful times, however, the need for self-defence training waned, and T'ai-Chi was taught mainly within the family, first of all to the teachers' children, and then to seriously interested students. In this way, different styles of T'ai-Chi evolved, and were named after the families that practised them. The Chen style, the Yang style and the Wu style continue to be practised today. Through the generations, countless students went on to change the styles according to their level of understanding and experience of T'ai-Chi.

Grandmaster Chen sharing the secrets of the T'ai-Chi of the Iron Ball with me.

When I spoke recently with Wu Zhongxian, a master of T'ai-Chi Wudang style, on the subject of longevity, I was not surprised to learn that his thoughts on the subject were the same as those of a grandmaster of T'ai-Chi Yang style, and a grandmaster of T'ai-Chi Chen style. They all agreed that longevity is not dependent upon the style you choose to practise, but on how much you practise your T'ai-Chi in accordance with the T'ai-Chi Classics (see page 141), and your diligence in committing your heart to the art. Do you love T'ai-Chi and enjoy T'ai-Chi with all your heart, body, mind and spirit? If you do, you have discovered the secret of longevity.

They all concurred, as well, that Yin, Yang and Tao were the three T'ai-Chi Classical Principles that were fundamental to the teachings of all the different schools and styles of T'ai-Chi. Whichever style you learn, the most important thing to remember is that you embody these principles.

When I think back to my visit to China, I feel a sense of immense gratitude to Grandmaster Chen Qingzhou for welcoming me into his family, and for introducing me to

Grandmaster Chen trying out the Rainbow T'ai-Chi idea of using tan-tien to sweep the floor.

his friends and relatives in the village. He was born in Chen village, went to the village school, married there and became a grandparent there. Everywhere we went, people acknowledged him not only as a great T'ai-Chi Master but as a wise counsellor, a calligraphic master (testified by his magical art on the doorways of most of the village houses) and friend to everyone. His happiness and laughter still fill me with joy when I think of his incredible sense of community and respect for human beings.

I found I was able to share my experiences of T'ai-Chi with him. I explained how I see T'ai-Chi offering precious gems of wisdom that will help modern man transform stress into creative opportunities for personal growth. I even got him to try out the Rainbow T'ai-Chi idea of applying the movements to simple actions such as sweeping the floor! At 76 years of age, he demonstrated a childlike innocence and purity that made him ever ready to play and learn.

As Grandmaster Chen Qingzhou, who represents the nineteenth generation of the Chen style of T'ai-Chi, said of my development of Rainbow T'ai-Chi: 'After more than thirty years of practice, you are evolving your own style naturally, combining all the best that you have learned from different masters. You have a natural gift from Heaven and you are bringing a new essence into the application of T'ai-Chi.'

With global concern about environmental damage growing daily, T'ai-Chi can provide a ray of hope for the world. If more people could slow down in order to sense their energetic connections with Nature, they would naturally come to respect Nature and naturally find more peaceful, harmonious and energy-conserving ways to live their daily lives.

Introduction

太極乃先根而生陰陽之母
動靜之機動之則分靜之則合
專心致志盡心探討深研
漸入佳境

陳氏太極拳
十九代人
陳慶州題

二〇〇〇年七月十二日于中國溫縣

Why do millions of people practise T'ai-Chi? I believe the main reason is because T'ai-Chi brings them improved health and a sense of rejuvenation. T'ai-Chi Form is a kind of meditation in movement, which can be practised by people of all abilities and ages, from seventeen upwards. The gentle exercises are based on the inherent flow of the limbs, arteries and muscles, using clear and tested Taoist principles. The gliding movements help to reduce stress and to train the mind to still itself, even in action. The term 'T'ai-Chi' means 'River of Chi Energy which flows unceasingly in a balanced state of harmony and happiness.'

The Tao of T'ai-Chi: Pure Nature Philosophy

Wise T'ai-Chi teachers and both ancient and modern-day medical scholars have concentrated on maintaining health and preventing disease. Illnesses, according to Taoist philosophy, are caused by emotional, physical and mental excesses. The Taoists have long believed that depression, for example, can cause stomach ulcers and indigestion, and this has been proved by modern medical science. Anger causes the liver to malfunction. Sadness creates stagnation and tightness in the lungs. Fear disturbs the functioning of the kidneys and bladder. To improve health, the Taoists advocate finding peace through the natural balancing of emotional, physical and mental activity. The art of T'ai-Chi slows a person down so that they can tap into this natural, universal chi and absorb it into their whole person as a nurturing and balancing force.

As many years of research have shown, T'ai-Chi practice helps to improve posture and strengthen the lower back and legs. It also lowers blood pressure and regulates circulation. The exercises balance the chi energy (or vital force) and condition the breathing and immune system. They also alleviate depression by centring the

This message reads, 'T'ai-Chi is the mother of Yin and Yang, movement and stillness. It is expansive when you move and contracts when you are still. When you keep your study and practice consistent and steady you will be able to climb to the highest in the field of endeavour of your choice.' My signature appears on the right-hand side and the signature of Grandmaster Chen Qingzhou is on the left.

practitioner emotionally, physically and mentally. The slow and gentle exercises have been found to increase awareness and appreciation of one's creative talents.

There are generally thought to be three main kinds of chi. There is chi in the human body, which relaxes the sinews and revitalizes the blood. Then there is the earth chi that can flow through the body into the joints. Chi from the heavens sensitizes the sensory organs. In T'ai-Chi, these three chi energies are linked together in many movements. You will see this, for example, at the beginning of Part Three of the Rainbow T'ai-Chi Form, 'Heaven, Humanity and Earth: Finding the Circle of Life'.

What Is 'Chi'?

According to Chinese philosophy, all illnesses are due to an imbalance of chi. When your chi is weak because you have been overworking and you feel tired and stressed, its flow becomes disharmonious and you become vulnerable to disease. When you are angry, your chi is aroused and you may commit regrettable actions. When you are happy, your chi is strong and smooth-flowing. When you are sad or anxious, your chi depletes. When you feel frightened, your chi is confused. Chinese medicine offers us many different ways of transforming an imbalance of chi – through T'ai-Chi and Chi Kung, diet, acupuncture and herbal medicine.

In this book, the term 'chi' is used to mean 'the rejuvenating vital force that exists in all life'. Whenever people slow down to 'tune' themselves, they have access to this energy. Most important of all, the intention of the practitioner guides the chi. We guide the chi with the clear intention of improving our health, and so it goes into personal self-development. In India it is known as 'prana', elsewhere it is often referred to as 'life force'. Chi

can be stored, channelled, recycled and transformed into different forms. The Rainbow T'ai-Chi Form helps to align earth chi, human chi and heavenly chi, and in this way restores the balance of energy in the whole person.

What Are Yin, Yang, Tao and T'ai-Chi?

Yin represents the receptive/feminine principle. Yang represents the assertive/masculine principle. When Yin and Yang join together, they become one, and this state of oneness is the Tao. The movement of this Yin and Yang towards oneness is called T'ai-Chi.

We also see Yin as the earth principle, Yang as the Heaven principle, and T'ai-Chi as the human moving between heaven and earth. In T'ai-Chi, the ideas of heavenly chi, earth chi and human chi are very important. When you have practised T'ai-Chi Chuan for some years, you feel that your every movement is part of the movement of the universe. It is as if you suddenly wake up to the fact that you are a tiny element in an ecstatic cosmic dance. The stretching of your arms is Yang/expansive, like the billions of stars that stretch across the galaxy so slowly and powerfully. The withdrawal of your arms is Yin/contracting, similar to the way we know universes spiral inward to a centre.

Practising flotation at the Rainbow T'ai-Chi School, Devon.

What Is the Purpose of this Book?

It is my wish to share with you my understanding of the ways in which you can improve your health and vital force through the practice of Rainbow T'ai-Chi. Many of the Rainbow T'ai-Chi topics included in this book, such as internal *Push Hands*, are not covered by other schools of T'ai-Chi, nor do they appear in book or video form anywhere else. There is no other book or school that demonstrates how to practise T'ai-Chi in water.

Most books and schools of T'ai-Chi either focus on the T'ai-Chi connection with 'Chuan' ('Outer Martial Arts application') or on the fitness and relaxation aspect of T'ai-Chi. While this book demonstrates the value of T'ai-Chi as a relaxation technique, it also stresses that relaxation is the result of an internal attunement to chi. When you watch the sea rolling on to the shore, you do not have to make the waves come in to feel relaxed. It just happens. You slow down, lie on the beach and let the sound of the gentle waves relax you. You feel happy in that relaxed state. T'ai-Chi tunes you in to the natural way in which relaxation happens inside your body. The rivers and seas of relaxation begin inside you and naturally express themselves externally in the way your body moves.

This book shows you how to achieve this graceful flow of movement through Aqua T'ai-Chi. I first recognized the connection between Rainbow T'ai-Chi principles and the flotation tank about fifteen years ago. Today, it has been proved through countless research programmes that flotation tanks are remarkably effective tools for combating pain and stress, unhealthy habits and addictions, and are even good for weight loss and improving athletic performance. In Aqua T'ai-Chi, this state of fluid awareness is taken one step further. People not only experience the wonderful sensation of lying peacefully in water, but are also able to continue feeling it when they are in motion, on land as well as in water. We like to practise centring exercises in the water to keep people 'grounded'.

How You Can Benefit from Rainbow T'ai-Chi Practice

Whether you are a beginner or an advanced student, you can use the movements as a mirror to show you who you truly are, and to explore the dimensions of your creative chi energy, rather than just mechanically following the instructions. In this way, you will be able to tap into more chi energy, and channel it to improve your health and make you feel rejuvenated.

The Rainbow T'ai-Chi Story

The Rainbow T'ai Chi Form is a story. Part One finds you 'On the Plains', heeding the call to return home. Then, gradually, you are guided up 'To the Mountain' on the journey to find your true self. And when you find your true self, your destiny appears as 'Heavenly Chi, Human Chi and Earth Chi' unite to show you the Circle of Life. The last part brings you to a sense of fulfilment through serving others. These themes are echoed in the lives of many successful people today, and the Rainbow T'ai-Chi Story points your way to success.

The Rainbow T'ai-Chi way is like the rainbow in the sky. When it appears, it integrates the light (Yang), rain droplets (Yin) and spectrum of colours (Tao). It is always full of surprises! Every time you see a rainbow in the sky, thank nature for showing you the Dance of T'ai-Chi between Heaven and Earth!

The Colours of the Rainbow T'ai-Chi Form

Each colour of the rainbow has its own significance as the story of the journey unfolds.

Violet

Rainbow T'ai-Chi increases your natural self-healing ability.
By seeing your Rainbow T'ai-Chi Form as a healing dance of Yin, Yang and Tao, you help to increase the circulation of chi energy in your body. You can also tune in to the chi and channel it for chi-healing purposes. My background in healing with chi energy started with my father and was later reinforced by studying with chi healing masters such as Dr Pang Ming of China.

Indigo

Rainbow T'ai-Chi builds your confidence in yourself as a leader.
Through the practice of breathing chi into your tan-tien your gut instincts will naturally be more acute, and you will feel more centred as a leader both in your business and in your social life. My leadership training can be traced back to the time I spent living in spiritual centres and communities throughout the world. In these places, I found myself integrated with the group dynamics of community living balanced with individual participation. I started newsletters to help facilitate the flow of chi in these communities. This flow of chi ensured that the interaction between Yin and Yang, especially in large meetings where there were hundreds of people, was experienced at a heart-centred level.

Blue

Rainbow T'ai-Chi helps you to be more peaceful.
By paying keen attention to certain elements in your practice, such as the spaces between the physical movements, you open yourself up to discover infinite peace. Your mind will naturally quieten down to meditate or concentrate without any effort on your part.

The blue energy of peace and clarity showed me the meditative side of T'ai-Chi. This has also revealed itself to me in some peaceful places I have visited, such as the the Krishnarmurti Foundation in Benares, Bonfin in southern France, and Zhineng Chi Kung Centre in China. Practising T'ai-Chi in the presence of the Bodhi tree and the River Ganges was an unforgettable experience – especially trying to find inner peace while being aggravated by hundreds of flies! I discovered that the smaller and more irritable the 'teacher' is, the more you will find that smiles of different sizes bubble up inside you: small smiles, medium-sized smiles, and large smiles that float you away into limitless peace. Even insects respect chi and calm down!

Green

With regular Rainbow T'ai-Chi practice, you become a natural magnet for harmony and prosperity.
Practising Rainbow T'ai-Chi outdoors, ideally next to a tree or with natural music playing in the background, is relaxing and will naturally guide you towards a rewarding relationship with Nature. Growing vegetables will also help you with this. Nature shows us how to experience small, beautiful movements within larger, beautiful movements. Once you can do this, your practice of the Rainbow T'ai-Chi Form will truly be a silent communion with the Nature Elements of Air, Fire, Water, Wood, Metal and Earth, and will bring you abundant surprises.

Yellow

Enlighten your work environment with Rainbow T'ai-Chi.
You can wake up the wise artist within you in the Rainbow T'ai-Chi movements, even in your place of work. I have practised T'ai-Chi in offices and found T'ai-Chi connections with light bulbs, calculating machines,

folding machines, photocopiers, guillotines, book-binding machines and even the carpets! The chi energy seemed to transform everything it touched into a self-realization exercise. I saw parallels between the Yin, Yang, T'ai-Chi and Tao principles and the artificial world. But, on reflection, can anything that is created or invented be separated from the Laws of Yin and Yang? When I first worked in an office, after leaving school, I was rapidly promoted to managerial level. Learning how to use resources at the ripe time and with skill, in any work place, was a very grounding and enriching experience for me.

Orange

Enjoy Rainbow T'ai-Chi as a tool for personal transformation.

By being relaxed and open to the lightness within you during your practice, you will feel peaceful smiles bubble up inside. These can accumulate into a waterfall of chi energy, making you feel ecstatic. Ever since I was a child, I have been interested in the comical side of life. I saw how comedians were using the Yin, Yang and Tao principles on a very human level to transform negative situations into positive and explosive laughter. I even went to comedy clubs to test and improve my skill, and to learn how to flow with audiences who did not even practise T'ai-Chi!

Rose Red

Rainbow T'ai-Chi heartbeat listening is great for improving your physical performance.

You can use T'ai-Chi to increase your stamina and enjoy doing more of the things you love. In Chinese medical theory, the heart meridian is the governor of all channels. This is particularly true at the level of human interaction – the heart governs all channels of communication!

How to Use this Book

Feel the exercises as you try them out. When you are receptive to this idea, your body will be able to assimilate the exercises and remember the movements more efficiently. You will be reminded again and again throughout the book to feel the exercises from your heart and tan-tien. The mind, with its need to understand the meaning of the movements, can play its part later.

Slow down to digest each sequence. Practise slowly and patiently. There are multi-dimensional layers in each sequence on which to meditate while you are doing and learning the movements. After your practice, pause for a while and let it sink into you.

Practise each movement at least 5-10 times before moving on. The sequence is like a piece of music. You have to hear the deeper layers. Every time you engage with it, you reach another layer. Limitless layers of insight await you.

Read the meditative poems and exercises aloud. The words I write must first pass through my lips. You can enjoy assimilating the words more when you read them aloud. In every chapter, there are principles, ideas and poems accompanying the instructions for the exercises.

Orient yourself with the elements of Nature. The movements of T'ai-Chi also follow the compass directions of the I Ching philosophy. Each direction corresponds with an element of Nature. Early T'ai-Chi practitioners learned to commune with the spirits of Kun/Earth in the north, Tian/Heaven in the south, Li/Fire in the east, Kan/Water in the west; Chen/Thunder in the north-east, Soon/Wind in the south-west, Tui/Lake in the south-east, Ken/Mountain in the north-west.

This may help to explain how practitioners can understand the principles behind some movements in this

Co-operation between Earth, humanity and heavenly chi energy presences.

book, such as *Fair Lady Works at Shuttles*. When you face north-west, you meditate on '...return to the Mountain within you and find infinite peace'. And when you face the south-west, 'You ride upon the Wind and flow with whatever Destiny brings you'.

Jot down any questions or insights. You may be inspired to write something down, although it may not make sense at the time. Inspiration is like a seed. It takes time to grow. Let me know how you get on. Use each sequence as a meditative affirmation of the natural Taoist philosophical principles to develop a more balanced and rejuvenating approach to human activity.

Four Dimensions of T'ai-Chi Learning

The first dimension is what beginners usually go through when they start T'ai-Chi. They have a one-dimensional view of what they are learning – most often from the perspective of trying to get the physical technique correct. They may even have an inner judge, as well, that has a critical view of their progress. After some months of regular practice, this narrow point of view does change, and students begin to see that they are, in fact, making progress, even though they know they have more work to do on their T'ai-Chi Form. They start to have two points of view about their experience. Part of them thinks that they are making progress and feels good and relaxed after practising. Another part sometimes begins criticizing. When you hold these two parts together, uniting the Yin/negative and the Yang/positive as in the *Grasp the Sparrow's Tail* sequence, you see them mirroring each other, playing a tug-of-love/tug-of-war game with each other. Finally, they are transformed into a third creative energy that is linked to the third dimension. In the third dimension, you let yourself relax into a peaceful, non-

judgemental place. Following on from there, in the *Single Whip/Standing like a Tree* sequence, you may be able to experience the fourth dimension wherein the harmonious chi flows naturally, connecting the earth energy with your human energy and the sky energy. When some T'ai-Chi masters get to this point, they see the whole T'ai-Chi Form embodied in these simple first few sequences.

The Rainbow T'ai-Chi Form as a Journey of Self-Discovery

This journey is partly based on my research and study of the T'ai-Chi Form and Classics, but it also comes from my experience over three decades of learning and teaching this art. Many T'ai-Chi masters agree that if you have been practising T'ai-Chi for a long time, you start to embody the T'ai-Chi philosophy and principles, so that essentially, it mirrors who you are, where you have been, and what you consider to be the purpose of your life. The T'ai-Chi Form is my friend, teacher, guide, lover and partner for life. If I want to know where I am within myself, I have only to look at my T'ai-Chi movements and I see it unfolding before my very eyes. Body language always reflects your state of mind and emotion, but it is even more profoundly apparent when the T'ai-Chi movements slow you down so that you can see where you are.

The nearest thing that a man can understand about the experience of birth is perhaps carrying a project around for nine months. Well, this baby book project has been long overdue, because I have been carrying it for more than thirty years! I have enjoyed the labour, and here it is, just for you! Take care of the Rainbow T'ai-Chi Form; it is something precious that is passed down to you. I have spent most of my life growing it, and now it is yours, too. *Be* it, and *do* it. Have fun learning!

Part One

On the Plains:

'The Calling to Return Home'

T'ai-Chi is the story of Yin, the feminine, searching for union with Yang. This yearning for union is within every human soul. An ancient feeling, a calling that will not stop till everyone has heard its voice. This desire for oneness is a desire for Unity in Diversity. This feeling is the sound of 'we': we – the people, we – the animals, we – the earth; the first note has been sounded. 'Let us return to the source, the source of chi': this feeling has echoed for thousands of years in the hearts of humankind, animals, insects, flying creatures in the sky, in the cities, towns, villages, in the mountains, valleys, and plains, and all the universes beyond.

The calling has gone forth: 'Come, it is the ripe time for us to return home.' Let us join the Dance of Yin and Yang searching for the T'ai-Chi flow, melting in the Tao, and come back to the beginning. With your feet shoulder-width apart, let us begin.

In the beginning was the void, wu-chi. In this stillness the pure chi energy moved in silence. This pure chi flowed into yin, the receptive, and yang, the assertive.

Pause for a while. Feel Yin and Yang flowing in harmony. Out of this harmony, the mind discovers that it is easy for its assertive side to let go and find stillness. In this quiet space, Yin mirrors Yang and Yang mirrors Yin. Then, chi issues forth from the tan-tien and gradually rises up to the heart. Sink into the earth, closer and closer to your heart. At the same time, allow there to be some space for chi to grow. ⌈Chi naturally rises up from the earth, rising to help you fulfil your highest aspirations⌋

Take a step towards the east. Gazing at the south-east, you discover the Laws of Yin and Yang. Yin attracts Yang, Yang attracts Yin. The Dance of Yin and Yang leading into T'ai-Chi. Yang supporting Yin like fire with water into creative steam, a joyful union of Yin and Yang. Yin and Yang rising, making love and reaching orgasm, creative

inspiration. Yin and Yang parting from each other, gracefully. Slowly rising up again, separate and yet together. When you sink slowly back into the tan-tien centre, feel a new stream of chi sweeping across the earth, awakening ancient memories. We have been together, like rolling waves in the sea of life, eternal songs of creation, from duality into oneness into duality.

Turn towards the west and feel the Five Elemental Spirits come to help you grow. Flowers of Light open to praise creation. Sink into the new roots of your being right now. Hold the inner baby/child in between your heart and belly. Release the old, advance and accept responsibility for your own health and happiness. ⌈The challenges in your life motivate you to find new ways of responding to the same old situations. You are a being of energy. An infinite abundance of health and happiness flow in you, right now.⌋

Go within, hear the inner voice of balance guiding you. A new turning point in your life. Hear the inner voice of stillness. Step forward into a new vision from your heart. ⌈Transform all negativity into creativity. That which you want so much, step forward to become one with it⌋

Know that there is also a time to let go and flow, and like water vapour rising up, you learn to rise and fall like gentle rain, bringing new hope to your daily life. Flow, and let the wheel of life turn within you.

Hear your inner voice from the stillness. Sink and melt into who you truly are and spiral your way through life. The gentle currents of chi carry you effortlessly into the future – confident, healthy and centred. Let the wisdom of the Five Elements guide you, empower you to go 100% for what you want. It is a time to release. Let go and sink in to gather more chi. Rise up to a new creative high. Sink into the tan-tien centre. ⌈The feminine principle keeps the stillness and simultaneously trusts the *masculine principle. To gather the force of goodness and conserve it in your internal organs is to live a long and prosperous life. By gently collecting the chi and channelling it into service, you will naturally move up the ladder of success. True leadership begins with being receptive to the needs of those you lead. Rejoice in their little victories.*

Sink down together. Lift each other up and return to the source. Let your gifts and talents be multiplied a thousandfold, trust the chi in your heart, body, mind and spirit.

In the course of the following pages we shall see how this story unfolds in the sequences of the T'ai-Chi Form.

Preparation for Learning T'ai-Chi Form
Heartbeat Listening: the 'Sensitive Heart' Approach

Some people think that the 'quiet heart' is a metaphor, as we might describe someone as being 'quiet at heart', meaning that they seem peaceful or retiring. But it is the actual sound of the heart beating – or rather the pauses in between the beats – that concerns us here. In this preparatory practice, we listen to our heartbeats. 'Heartbeat listening' has been found to produce many positive effects, including improved circulation and co-ordination. Many people who have high blood pressure find themselves calmer and their heartbeat rate back to normal after only about 10 minutes of heartbeat listening.

Movement becomes more graceful. As you give more space to your heart, it feels relaxed, accepted and at peace. When you feel more peaceful, you are able to think more clearly and make wiser decisions. You can also feel the chi energy circulate through the blood system to energize your internal organs. Research studies have found that heartbeat listening is more effective in relaxing participants into a peaceful pulse rate than mantric meditation.

Heartbeat Listening Exercise

1. Place your palm on your chest (to the left side, slightly above your breast) and see if you can trace your heartbeat. Do not 'hear' it with your ears; feel its rhythms, the valves opening and closing. Can you? Yes?

2. Next, listen to the pauses in between your heartbeats. Pauses? Yes, no matter how fleeting those pauses are, you need to follow them. These pauses help you to relax into the formless empty spaces – essential spaces, where you can feel the chi – before you begin practising the T'ai-Chi Form.

3. After about 5 minutes, you will feel a natural, tingling warmth in your palm and your chest. Allow yourself to concentrate on it and 'melt' your mind into it.

4. Be in this quiet, radiant space for another 5 minutes.

CHAPTER ONE

Begin the Endless Journey of Self-Discovery

POSTURE **1**

Preparation

T'ai-Chi is the story of Yin, the feminine, searching for union with Yang. This yearning for union is within every human soul. An ancient feeling, a calling that will not stop till everyone has heard its voice. This desire for oneness is a desire for Unity in Diversity. This feeling is the sound of 'we': 'we – the people, we – the animals, we – the earth'; the first note has been sounded. 'Let us return to the source, the sea of chi': this feeling has echoed for thousands of years in the hearts of humankind, animals, insects, flying creatures, in the cities, towns, villages, in the mountains, valleys, and plains, and all the universes beyond.

At the start of the journey, white reflects the transparency and purity of the beginning sequences of Rainbow T'ai-Chi Form.

A

1. You are facing north. Slowly open your feet about the width of your shoulders. Point both feet directly ahead. Place your feet parallel to each other. Put one palm on your heart and the other on your tan-tien. Your mind should be quiet. Pay attention to your breathing. Relax and enjoy the peaceful spaces in between your heartbeats, your in-breath and your out-breath. Do this for about 5 minutes.

Now, allow both of your palms to slide to the sides of your thighs.

2. Gradually move your elbows slightly outward and turn your wrists upward. Feel the spaces in between your fingers. They are moving slightly to feel the chi. Your palms are down **(A)**.

Keep your head and spine vertical. Relax your shoulders and allow your chest to be slightly hollow. Feel your heartbeat as the chi glows in the surrounding area. Gradually, sink your chi down to your navel (do this with your mind: simply feel the chi sinking down).

(For those who know them or who are interested in learning them, the 15 Fundamental T'ai-Chi Chi Kung Exercises are also recommended as part of your preparation.)

POSTURE 2
Beginning

The calling has gone forth: 'Come, it is the ripe time for us to return home now.' Let us join the Dance of Yin and Yang searching for the T'ai-Chi flow, melting in the Tao, and come back to the beginning. With your feet shoulder-width apart, let us begin.

In the beginning was the void, Wu-Chi. In this stillness the pure chi energy moved in silence.

A

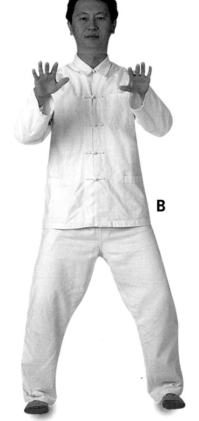

B

C

1. Feel a peaceful smile inside. Your arms should feel as if they are being controlled by a puppeteer above you. Strings attached to your wrists and elbows raise your arms upward to shoulder-height. The wrists and fingers are curved as your arms move up. Chi is felt all around you as you extend your fingers slightly **(A)**.

2. Bring back your arms by sinking your elbows a little **(B)**. As your elbows sink towards your body, let them glide down to your sides, fingers pointing downwards. Your wrists are carried down as if you are sinking into water, your fingertips floating.

3. You are in Posture 1 (p. 24) again **(C)**.

T'ai-Chi River Meditation

'T'ai-Chi' means 'River of Limitless Chi Energy'.
The scientists agree that even these dots – ... – are made of particles of energy. The spiritualists agree that everything is spirit. In T'ai-Chi we agree and take this one step further, to show how we can experience these facts in a relaxing way.

You may be feeling some stress right now. Perhaps something that has been at the back of your mind is disturbing you and making you feel worried. You may turn to a cup of tea or coffee or a cigarette to help you deal with your anxiety.

A thought can be simply a dot in your mind; this whole galaxy can also be just a dot if you go far away from it and look back. If your thoughts are bound by a lot of stress, that will tighten and harden up different parts of your body. Shoulders and neck, for example, may feel stiff. Arteries and veins also may harden. And more health problems ensue.

So, the mind begins to think of escaping from this stress. If there is a lot of stress, the final answer may be, 'How about a holiday?' And until that can be arranged, it may mean, 'In the meantime, I will grit my teeth and suffer the anxieties my problem brings... including the daily insults, bruises and pain of work and relationships.'

Or... your mind could choose the T'ai-Chi Formless Meditative way of dealing with your stress, *right now*!

After all, even if you go for a holiday, you may find that it is simply a temporary form of escape before the stress hits you again on your return.

The T'ai-Chi River Meditation can be done *right now*, anywhere. Even when you are on holiday or at work. So, are you here, right now?... Okay, shall we go into it?

To understand this T'ai-Chi River, we must return to the definition of T'ai-Chi, 'The Limitless River of Chi Energy'. The mind is limited in its perception of the problem and possible solution. The mind says, 'I feel... because... because...
I think.. .because... because...

However, it finds it difficult to realize that the way to find a solution is
to *let this limitless river of energy come into being*. The solution begins when you *become soluble*!
To achieve this, the mind first of all needs to educate itself, and calmly recede into
the background so that the flowing, limitless river of energy can come into your consciousness, right now.

It is as if you are by a river... your thoughts float by you. Feelings may come up... just let them float by you without adding more thoughts or feelings to them. The thoughts are like leaves floating on that river. Some of them look like pollutants... plastic bags, rubbish... let them go.

The more stressful the feelings are, the more they may try to stick to you. You think about them, you feel worried about worrying outcomes. And then, you feel worried that you are so worried. Although you may try not to show this, it is registered within your internal organs. You may end up sullen, moody... pacing round and round like a dog tied to a post.

So, you slow the mind down, right now, to acknowledge that there may be another way. Watch how the mind gently relaxes when it is no longer attached to any thoughts. At the same time, it does not try to escape from any thoughts floating by...

Feel the stillness in motion.

Mind quiet...naturally.

Transparent like water. Nowhere to go...feel you are now...here...

HOMEWORK **1**

1. Practise the *Heartbeat Listening* exercise on p. 23.
2. Go through the Preparation and Beginning postures slowly and carefully for 15 minutes a day. Practise every day until you become familiar with the feel of the chi energy.
3. Practise T'ai-Chi Walking (p. 181); it will help you with your T'ai-Chi steps.
4. If you would like to complement your study, and have access to the first Rainbow T'ai-Chi book, *15 Ways to a Happier You*, you may find the sections on Cognitive Perception/Recognitive Perceptions (pp. 19-20) useful at this stage. You should also practise the First Chi Kung and Second Fundamental T'ai-Chi exercises.

CHAPTER TWO
Follow the Heart's Way to Peace and Contentment

Pause for a while. Feel Yin and Yang flowing in harmony. Out of this harmony, the mind discovers that it is easy for its assertive side to let go and find stillness. In this quiet space, Yin mirrors Yang and Yang mirrors Yin. Then, chi issues forth from the tan-tien and gradually rises up to the heart.

Sink into the earth, closer and closer to your heart. At the same time, allow there to be some space for chi to grow. Chi naturally rises up from the earth, rising to help you fulfil your highest aspirations.

POSTURE 3
Grasp the Sparrow's Tail, Ward-Off, Left

This pure chi flowed into Yin, the receptive, and Yang, the assertive.

1. Gradually shift most of your weight on to your left leg, bending your left knee and straightening your right knee. Relax the right side of your torso and turn your right foot on its heel towards the east. Keep your toes raised slightly **(A)**.

The bending of your left knee lowers the body; your right foot is now at right angles to your left foot. Your right palm is resting beside your thigh.

A

B

2. When you turn, turn your waist and thigh at the same time, so that your waist co-ordinates the whole movement. Turn towards the east, shifting your weight on to your right leg, and simultaneously raise your right hand, palm facing the earth, to the level of your right armpit (in front of your chest). Your left hand flows with the waist towards the right and the palm is facing up. Imagine you are holding a ball in between your palms. Your weight shifts to your right foot, so that your left is brought to its toes **(B)**.

3. Relax your right shoulder during this movement. Your eyes and head follow the movement of your waist and you now face north-east **(C)**.

4. Move your left hand slightly (about 15 degrees) towards the left. Take a step towards the north with your left foot, the heel touching the ground first. Bend your left knee, and gradually shift 70% of your weight on to your left foot while turning the right side of your upper torso to the left. Let the right foot follow the turning of the waist. Raise your left hand to a point parallel with your chest, palm facing your chest and fingers pointing slightly down **(D)**.

5. Gradually lower your right hand to the side of your right thigh. The right foot is now at 45 degrees towards the north. Your left foot is directly pointing north **(E)**.

6. Gently shift most of your weight on to your left leg until your right foot is brought to its toes. Simultaneously, turn your right arm with your waist, so that the right elbow is just beside your left palm **(F)**.

7. Take a step with your right foot towards the east. Sink your right elbow and as you turn your waist, turn your left palm to face down. Simultaneously, turn your right palm to face up. Relax your shoulders as you are performing these movements. Your eyes accompany the gradual turn **(G)**.

POSTURE 4

Ward-off, Right

Take a step towards the east. Gazing south-east, you discover the laws of Yin and Yang.

1. Facing east, with your right palm facing you and your left palm facing the right palm, shift 70% of your weight on to your bent right leg. Your upper torso is now in the *Ward-off, Right* posture. As you shift the weight on to your right leg, turn the left foot from your waist so that it is pointing 45 degrees towards the east.

A

2. Your right elbow is lowered slightly, with the right palm facing your chest, and your left palm faces outward, with the left elbow down, midway in the space between your right wrist and elbow **(A)**.

POSTURE 5

The Rollback

Yin attracts Yang. Yang attracts Yin. The Dance of Yin and Yang leads into T'ai-Chi.

Rock and Roll into Laughter

Is the feeling hard, like rock, or is it the Rolling River that you follow when trouble comes your way?
Or, perhaps, you stay with the tension between the two.
Go with the Rock and Roll rhythm,
find what you really need;
  Just as the river bed needs her rocks to be who she is,
    the hard situations in your life are there to remind you to relax
    and softly find the humorous, 'upside-down' side to what has just
    happened to you.

A

B

1. From Posture 4, relax your right arm, turn your upper torso slightly to the right (south-east). Extend your right arm slightly **(A)**.

2. From A, turn your left arm from your waist and make a circular movement in a clockwise direction **(B)**.

POSTURE 6

Grasp the Sparrow's Tail, Press

Yang supports Yin, like fire and water into creative steam, a joyful union of Yin and Yang.

Handling the Path of Wisdom
You handle the pressures of your daily life by turning to your hands for the answer.
Let your right palm (representing your masculine aspects)
learn to support your left elbow
(representing your feminine aspects).
Female and male playing together until both melt into Oneness,
the Ecstatic Light shines through the Way they hold each other.
Hand in hand, wrist upon wrist,
they walk and dance into the Days and Nights.

1.Turn your right hand so that the palm comes around to the left side of your abdomen **(A)**.

A

2. Turn your right wrist and waist simultaneously towards the north-east while holding your left hand, palm up, near your left ear. Your left knee is bent and receives all your weight as your upper torso and arms swing in slow motion to the north-east **(B)**.

B

Shift all your weight very slowly forward on to left foot, pulling your arms slowly towards your left, from your tan-tien. Feel the wavy space all around as you turn your arms.

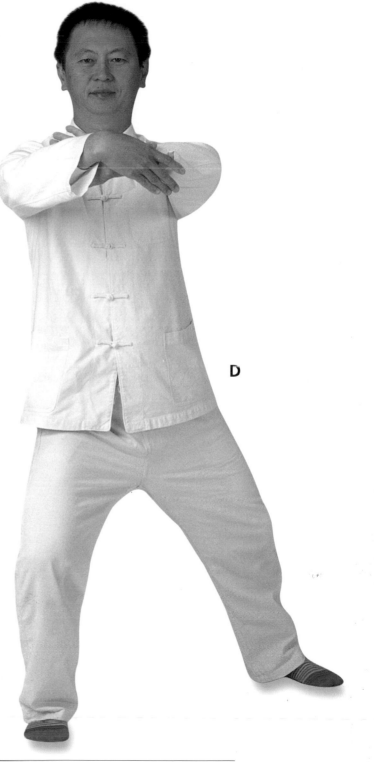

C

D

3. Glide your left wrist down to fall gently into place with the right wrist **(C)**.

4. With both wrists locked together gently, move forward towards the east. Simultaneously, 70% of your body's weight should slowly shift on to the right foot. Press forward and slightly upward, keeping your arms relaxed. You are facing east **(D)**.

POSTURE 7

Grasp the Sparrow's Tail, Push

Yin and Yang rising, making love and reaching orgasm, creative inspiration. Yin and Yang parting from each other, gracefully. Slowly rising up again, separate and yet together. When you sink slowly back into the tan-tien centre, feel a new stream of chi sweeping across the earth, awakening ancient memories. We have been together, like rolling waves in the sea of life, eternal songs of creation, from duality into oneness into duality.

1. Both arms and wrists are at shoulder height. Withdraw all your weight on to your left foot while separating your hands. Your hands should open very, very slowly, as you glide your fingers, lower arms and wrists outwards **(A)**.

2. Gradually shift 70% of your weight on to your right leg and push forward with both arms and upper torso. Your arms are bent and move as part of your whole body. Both palms slide upward, facing forward, while your elbows should be at 45 degrees **(B)**.

A

B

HOMEWORK 2

1. Practise the *Grasp the Sparrow's Tail* sequence for 15 minutes.

2. To complement your practice, use the story of the journey for contemplation.

3. How do you feel about the physical movements of this sequence?
   Which parts make you feel what you feel?

4. Write down some daily observations about your everyday body movements:
   a) Notice what happens to those awkward T'ai-Chi body movements when you become conscious of them without being judgemental of them.
   b) Be aware of how your body naturally sways in micro-millimetres, even when you are sitting quietly or standing still.

CHAPTER THREE
You Deserve to Succeed Right Now

POSTURE 8
Single Whip

Turn towards the west and feel the Five Elemental Spirits come to help you grow. Flowers of Light open to praise creation. Sink deep into the new roots of your being, right now.

Success is yours, right now. Be as a tree, firmly rooted, holding a single point of concentration. Simultaneously, you are as open as the sky, free to flower and bear the fruits of the success you truly deserve.

White shifts naturally into the green of the Single Whip sequence, which expresses Nature's harmony, health and balance, helping you to root yourself in your values and principles.

A

B

C

1. Shift most of your weight on to your left foot, then turn on your right heel. Turn your toes inward as far as possible. Simultaneously, hold your arms parallel, slightly bend the elbows and turn your body as far as possible to the rear left (south-west) corner **(A, B)**.

2. Very gently, as you shift most of your weight onto your right leg, bring both arms back to hold an imaginary ball in between your palms **(C)**.

36

D

E

3. Gently raise your left palm to open up, and at the same time, turn your left foot on its heel and raise your foot to step towards the west **(D, E)**.

4. Step into a square formation facing west. Shift 70% of your weight onto the left foot. Simultaneously, stretch your elbow and keep your right palm in the same position **(F)**.

F

G

H

I

5. As you turn your left palm to face forward, bring the fingers of your right hand together to form a bird's beak **(G,H,I)**.

The T'ai-Chi Tree

You stand in front of a tree

Your heart is open with humility; the tree is one in spirit with you.

Feel the trunk as your waist – great strength and

majestic presence are here to stay;

Your arms are her thick branches, spreading out further and further into the sky.

Feel the left palm open like the broadest leaf of all leaves,

Your fingers stretch, longer and longer... and longer, into limitlessness

On your right, you hold the Five Elemental Spirits –

they have danced the dance of timelessness, long before you were born.

You see and feel the warmest wind and most frightening storms;

You have been there to taste the purest rain

drenching you right into the core of your being

The fiery skies of golden orange and hues of purple and crimson blue have burnt the forests, all except

for this great tree;

Your right fingers collect together and you sink so deep

you forget everything and disappear.

Are you the eagle's beak

or are you the penetrating roots of a 10,000-year-old tree,

or are you perhaps both?

Hold the stillness that is here now, become this silence that is louder than all the thunderclaps ever heard

by human ears.

Your feet feel the chi of this old, old friend, this earth you call home.

You are as transparent as the sap that rises

up the ancient roots of this tree, Humanity.

Come forth, bringer of new life, kindness, generosity, peace and hope.

You stand with us through innumerable crises and hurts, warts and all;

You teach us the way of Nature, take all our negatives from us,

transform, decompose and recycle our emotions,

thank you for sharing your enriching qualities of goodness with us always, dearest unknown friend of all,

thank you.

POSTURE 9

Lift Hands and Hold Your Inner Baby/ Child Playing the Lute with Left Hand Sequence

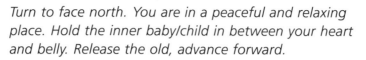

Turn to face north. You are in a peaceful and relaxing place. Hold the inner baby/child in between your heart and belly. Release the old, advance forward.

1. While sinking your weight gradually on to your left foot, turn your upper torso slightly to the right **(A)**.

A

B

C

2. Resting on your left leg, raise your right foot and turn it in a semicircle, letting it come down lightly on the heel. The right heel is perpendicular to the left heel **(B)**.

3. Your arms should be turning together with your right foot. Your arms turn inward so that the palms face each other. Slowly, bring your arms closer together until your right hand is in front, aligned with your right leg, and your left hand is back directly opposite your right elbow **(C)**.

Be in Pre-Birth Chi Right Now

When you open your arms to limitless energy in the universe, feel pre-birth chi in between your palms –
the purest essence in you is here now.
It was there before you came into this world;
Your body remembers this lovely warmth all round.
This long-forgotten memory of being in an ocean of chi
in your mother's womb awakens,
Although darkness was all around, too, you felt safe in this protective, watery home.
Every cell of your being now remembers this feeling.

Pre-birth chi encompasses you right now,
A ceaseless flow of beauty and innocence cares for you in fathomless fluids,
Quiet presences of pre-birth chi holding you, helping you grow inch by inch,
even when you came out into a loud and hard world.
Cradling you in every second, every minute and every hour of your life, every day.

Sometimes you forget this fluid warmth and tingling joy –
this memory seems so distant and far away from your neediness,
your need for warmth, sometimes met by the harsh world of hurtful rejections.
No one seems to understand or care about how you feel.
Your inner child screams out, unquenchable thirst for love and attention;
Inner walls alienate you, locking you in imaginary prisons.

You hold this part of you in your arms.
You hold the child's breath with all your heart, no matter how lifeless it seems to be.
All the years of anger, frustration and loud sounds may have made this child distrustful. Keep holding on
with utmost gentleness. Let all feelings come up naturally.
Gently sway your arms with tenderness.
You may think, 'I can't... I can't. It is too painful.'
Within these painful feelings lies the answer.
Within the Yin of pain, the Yang of freedom and peace awaits you.
Like snow melting slowly in the early morning sun, your arms hold
the most beautiful feelings of purity and innocence,
Let go and feel your whole being one with you.

You are at one with your inner child.

As flower buds open in the early morning hours of spring.

You feel this spontaneous smile coming up from deep within.

It comes up like a little stream...

Patiently nourish it with your attention.

This peaceful feeling beckons you to dive into it even more deeply.

Let yourself melt deeper and deeper into it.

Your heart and lungs flow in rhythm to the movement of your arms.

Be-hold. Open yourself to be carried by the 'Be-loved', this deep, pure chi.

You are the Beloved One within you!

Peaceful smiles slowly bubble up in you right now.

POSTURE **10**

Lean Forward/Shoulder Responsibility

A

Accept responsibility for your own health and happiness.

The challenges in your life motivate you to find new ways of responding to the same old situations.

You are a being of energy. An infinite abundance of health and happiness flow in you, right now.

1. Relax your right foot and let it rest on the floor. Gradually sink your right arm down, letting the right palm, facing downwards, fall gently, in slow motion. As your right palm glides down, transfer your weight slowly to your right foot. Your left foot should slide towards the heel of your right **(A)**.

POSTURE 11
Stork Spreads Wings

Go within, hear the inner voice of balance guiding you. A new turning point in your life. Hear the inner voice of stillness.

Following from the tree, spreading itself into the sky, the stork spreads its wings and lifts the dancer up into the blue attributes of freedom, peace and clarity.

1. Keep your left palm, which should be positioned in front of the right shoulder, still. You are facing north **(A)**. Slowly turn towards the left (west). Your left palm gradually glides down your upper right shoulder, as you raise your right arm to the side of your right ear **(B, C)**.

A

B

C

HOMEWORK 3

1. Get a bonsai tree or houseplant (if you are not sure how to care for it, please take the time to do some research).

2. When you practise your T'ai-Chi exercises, put the plant in front of you and silently feel respect for its presence. It is representative of Nature and will remind you how to be serene and rooted in your practice.

3. Write down any personal insights you may experience while practising the following sequences: *Single Whip, Playing the Lute/Hold your Inner Baby/Child, Lean Forward/Shoulder Responsibility* and *Stork Spreads Wings*.

4. List ten successful actions you have completed in the past month. They may be small projects, such as repairing something or doing some household chores you meant to do for some time.

5. Remember to practise holding your inner baby/inner child the next time you feel needy or lonely. How did you feel after doing it for 5-10 minutes?

6. List ten mini-projects you would like to do over the next month, and visualize them already completed.

CHAPTER FOUR

Grow Down Before Growing Up! Your Seed Ideas Are Taking Root, Right Now!

POSTURE 11B

Wheel Turning Sequence

Flow with the new energy cycle in your life, right now!

1. Slowly turn your arms towards the east from your tan-tien centre; feel it as the hub of a wheel, with your two arms as spokes. Your whole body moves towards your right side. The elbows are connected to the space around your tan-tien. Your left foot turns on the ball of your left heel **(A, B, C)**.

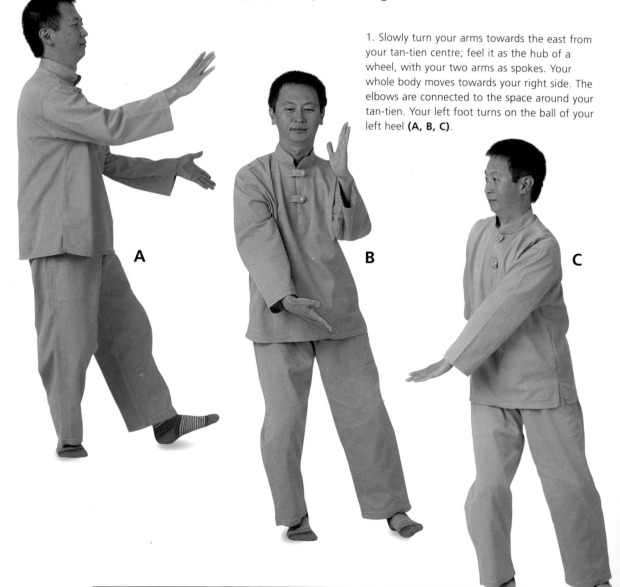

A

B

C

2. Turn your right arm around and sink your elbow to bring the right palm up towards your head **(D)**.

D

E

3. Tiptoe on your left foot. Your right palm should be at the side of your right ear **(E)**.

POSTURE 12

Brush Left Knee and Twist Step

Step forward towards the west into a new vision from your heart. Transform all negativity into creativity. Step forward to become one with your greatest desire.

1. With your weight still on your right foot, turn your waist slightly to the right, move your left thigh behind your left palm and step lightly forward into a square position. Your left palm brushes your left thigh lightly as your leg moves into position **(A)**.

A

B

2. Gradually shift 70% of your weight on to your left foot. Simultaneously, sink your right elbow and arm down so that it is positioned in front of your chest. You are facing west **(B)**.

POSTURE 13A
Lift Hands and Hold Your Inner Baby/Child Playing the Lute with Right Hand Sequence

Know that there is also a time to let go and flow, and like water vapour rising up, you learn to rise and fall like gentle rain, bringing new hope to your daily life. Flow, and let the wheel of life turn within you.

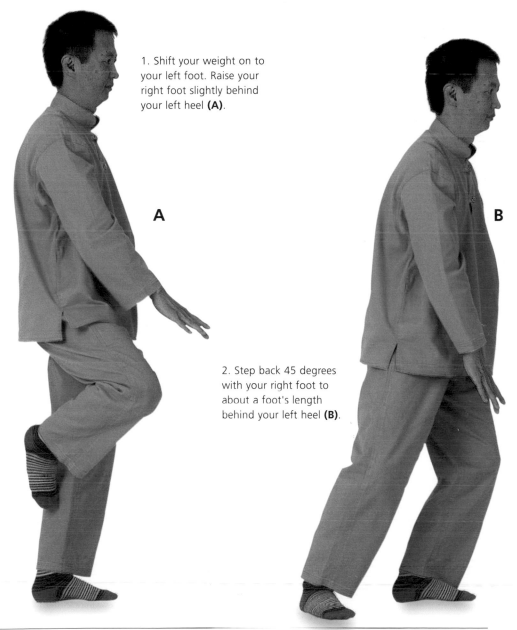

1. Shift your weight on to your left foot. Raise your right foot slightly behind your left heel **(A)**.

A

B

2. Step back 45 degrees with your right foot to about a foot's length behind your left heel **(B)**.

3. Shift your weight on to your right foot and raise both arms together up to chest level. Simultaneously, raise your left knee and sink your weight on to your right foot **(C, D, E)**.

C

D

E

F

4. At the same time, turn your upper torso slightly to the left. Your arms turn inward so that your palms face each other **(F)**.

POSTURE **13B**
Wheel Turning Sequence

Flow, and let the wheel of life turn within you.
Hear your inner voice of stillness. Sink and melt into who you truly
are and spiral your way through life.

1. Slowly turn your arms from your tan-tien centre; feel it as the hub of a wheel, and your two arms as spokes. Your whole body moves towards the right side. The elbows are connected to space around your tan-tien centre. Your left foot turns on the ball of your left heel **(A, B)**.

A

B

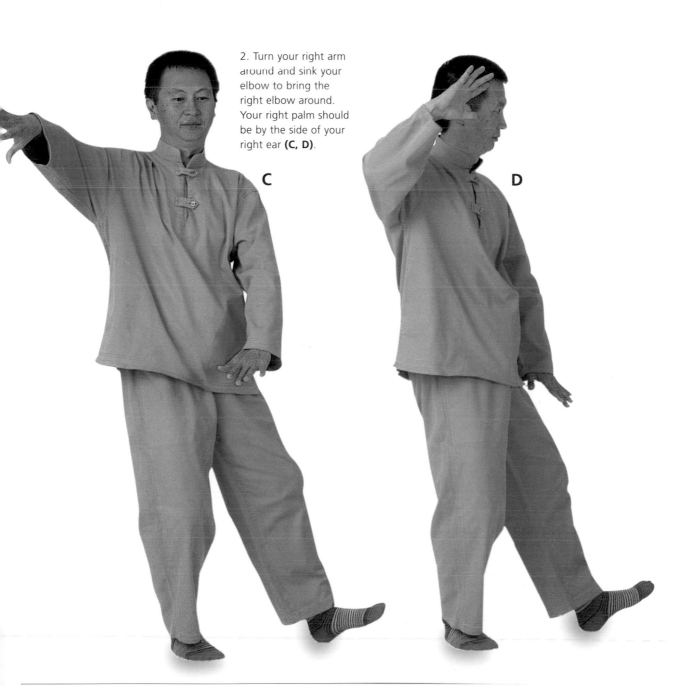

2. Turn your right arm around and sink your elbow to bring the right elbow around. Your right palm should be by the side of your right ear **(C, D)**.

C

D

POSTURE 13c
Brush Left Knee and Twist Step

*Step forward with confidence and let the gentle currents of chi carry
you effortlessly into the future.*

1. With your weight still on your right foot,
turn your waist slightly to the right, move your
left thigh behind your left palm and step lightly
forward into a square position. ('Square' sides
are based on the width of your shoulders.) Your
left palm brushes your left thigh lightly as your
leg moves into position **(A)**.

2. Gradually shift 70% of your weight
on to your left foot. Simultaneously,
sink your right elbow and arm down so
that they are positioned in front of your
chest. You are facing west again **(B)**.

A

B

HOMEWORK 4

1. Keep a diary of the seed-ideas and mini-project plans you started in Homework 3.

2. Note down the results you have managed to achieve so far (however small).

3. Do the following sequences: *Wheel Turning*, *Brush Left Knee and Twist Step*, and *Play the Lute with Right Hand*. Jot down any personal insights you may have gained from your practice.

4. What do you think the T'ai-Chi Principle of 'Effortless Action' means? Please cite five examples of this from your daily life. How, from your personal experience, do these ideas connect with personal communication in the work-place, in the family, and generally?

CHAPTER FIVE
You Are a Natural Leader. First, Lead Yourself

POSTURE **14**
Step Forward, Deflect Downward, Parry and Punch

Let the wisdom of the Five Elements guide you, and empower you to go 100 per cent for what you want. Empower yourself with the Spiralling Power of Creative Force in your tan-tien. Co-operate with Nature and meet the challenges in your daily life with humour. Let all negatives bring you closer to positive and creative changes, right now.

On a clear midnight, in an indigo sky, you will find the spiralling Parry and Punch *sequence connect to the spiralling star formations of the cosmos.*

1. You are facing west. Withdraw your weight from the front left foot, shifting it completely on to the right foot **(A)**.

A

B

C

2. At the same time, turn your waist towards the left (south-west) side and allow both arms to fall gently. Move your weight forward on to the left foot **(B)**.

3. Then, turn both elbows to raise them up, in a circular (clockwise) movement **(C)**.

4. Your left palm circles in front of your left ear. Co-ordinate this movement from your waist **(D)**. At the same time, shift your weight completely on to your left foot, take a step forward with your right foot (so that your feet are about shoulder width apart) and align your right foot to drop at an angle of 45 degrees facing north-west **(E)**.

5. Shift your weight on to the right foot **(F)**. Glide your palms down towards your right side, left palm on top of your right wrist, left palm facing down, right palm facing up **(G)**. With your left foot step forward one square of an imaginary grid. Shift 70% of your weight on to your left foot **(H)**.

D

E

F

G

H

I

J

6. With most of your weight still on your left foot **(I)**, lightly form a fist with your right palm facing up, under your left wrist **(J)**. Punch gently forward with your right hand sliding under your left palm **(K)**.

K

L

7. Your right fist and lower arm are turning like a screw, anti-clockwise. Slide your left palm and fingers down under your right elbow **(L)**.

Learning How to Lead Yourself Is Like Discovering How to Be a T'ai-Chi Dancer: a Student's Experience

Mandy had all the brilliant skills of a dancer. She had come to find out more about T'ai-Chi energy, and how it related to the energy of the dance. I asked her to share her experiences of dance techniques, and to explain what 'energy' meant to her. She hesitantly began by saying she was not good with words, but that she would try to impart what she had learned from her many years' training with different master dance instructors in France, Africa and England.

She told us that after the warm-ups, she experienced a sense of 'letting go', and that time passed very quickly. Her 'ego' disappeared and she felt effortless in her movements. Then she began to dance.

When she had finished, I shared my thoughts with her: 'Any of the movements you have just shown me – for example, when you open your arms like that – I can transform into an experience of chi through the arms.' (I copied what she had just done but in slow motion.) 'I need to slow the movements you did down to reconnect them back to the fluidity and spiralling chi. These aspects get missed out in the speed of modern-day dance rhythms. Try this for yourself and see. Do you feel the chi energy in the way I am doing it now?'

She nodded and added, 'I am also learning how to align my spine and be more conscious of my movements when I walk in daily life.'

I asked her to show me. She walked around with her spine upright and was careful with her footsteps. She said that she used to walk like a duck when she was doing ballet, and now, after working with other relaxing dance techniques, she walked in a more relaxed and confident way.

I proposed that we should add the T'ai-Chi principle of spiralling movement to her walk. 'Can you feel the layers of air under your feet? It is like substance; this chair and that chair are upholstered with different materials, and compare the hardness of this wall... feel all those different textures under your feet. Feel your foot spiral even before touching the floor.'

She paused and pressed her raised front foot in mid-air before touching the floor. I encouraged her to do this several times, and asked her, 'Can you feel that?' And she could. She could feel chi in her feet!

This fluidic space is so important in our daily movements. In T'ai-Chi, we co-ordinate the movements from the tan-tien centre and connect the actions to fluidity. This awareness allows us to be receptive to chi, as water is to electricity. The spaces between the footstep and the floor, the spaces between our thoughts, the spaces between an in-breath and an out-breath, and the spaces between heartbeats... these spaces take us into a Dance of Yin and Yang. This is what T'ai-Chi can do to add something special to the dancer in our daily living.

Any movement can be transformed into a T'ai-Chi Form movement. I showed Mandy how I would do ironing, vacuuming, sweeping, etc., in this way. She saw how easy and effortless the movements were while at the same time, electrifying chi was present in every movement, both with her arms and with her feet.

POSTURE 15
Withdraw and Push

It is a time to release. Let go and sink in to gather more chi. Rise up to a new creative high. Sink into your tan-tien centre. The feminine principle keeps the stillness and simultaneously trusts the masculine principle. To gather the force of goodness and conserve it in your internal organs is to live a long and prosperous life. By gently collecting the chi and channelling it into service, you will move yourself up the ladder of success naturally. True leadership begins with being receptive to the needs of those you lead. Rejoice in their little victories.

1. You are facing west. Open your right fist slowly (like a flower opening her petals) **(A)**.

A

B

2. The left palm slides from under the right elbow up the right lower arm and the arms separate from each other, gradually opening to the sides **(B)**.

3. Gently float both your arms down to the sides. Both arms come down as if they are holding a large water barrel **(C)**.

C

4. Simultaneously, shift 70% of your weight forward on to your right leg and push forward with both arms and upper torso **(D)**.

D

E

5. Your arms are bent and move as part of the whole body. Both palms slide upward, facing forward. Your elbows are at 45 degrees to the horizontal **(E)**.

POSTURE 16A

Cross Hands

You are now approaching the mountain, the second part of your journey. Your palms gradually gather chi from the earth. Chi accumulates naturally in your tan-tien. As chi energy is absorbed and begins to multiply, your chi sinks and opens to limitless, loving chi.

Chi energy multiplies a thousandfold when your actions come from a balance of Yin (feminine)/Yang (masculine) and Tao (creative) principles.

You allow the accumulated chi to be distributed and shared with those who are open and receptive. Your talents, skills and services flow like a new stream, in a small current at first, which picks up when it joins other streams of inspiring action groups. You are in a steady river of happy surprises and creative insights.

After reaching the highest peak, and coming down to earth, the T'ai-Chi dancer dives into rose red, glowing with love, beauty and courage.

1. You are facing north. Sink most of your weight gently on to your right foot **(A)**. Keep your left hand very still, and at the same time raise your right arm above your head, so that it crosses in front of your face with its palm facing outward. Slowly raise it above your head. Meanwhile, raise the front part of your left foot slightly, so that it rests lightly on the ball of the foot, and turn it so that it is at right angles to the direction you are facing **(B)**.

A

B

C

2. As your right arm comes down gently to the same level as the left hand, shift the weight of your body to your left foot and bring the right foot in so that it is parallel to the left **(C, D)**.

D

3. Sink both arms down together **(E)**.

E

F

G

4. Raise both arms up along the mid-line section of the body to cross at chest level **(F, G)**.

POSTURE 16B

Cross Hands

This beautiful chi naturally divides itself like fields of radiant flowers shining in the sun, whose seeds are scattered in the wind.

1. From the *Cross Hands* posture **(A)**, sink your weight on to the right foot, raise your left foot slightly on the ball of the foot and turn the left arm towards the left from the waist. At the same time, sink the right palm to the holding position in front of your tan-tien **(B)**.

A　　　　　**B**　　　　　**C**

2. Sweep your left arm around towards the north-east. Shift the weight of your body on to the right foot **(C)**.

3. When your left palm reaches out as far as it can, drop your left elbow slowly, bringing it back round **(D, E)**.

D

E

HOMEWORK 5

1. Go out into Nature, and collect five things to represent the Five Elements (fire, water, metal, earth and wood).
   Meditate on each one of them cognitively and write down your inner experiences.

2. Do the following sequences: *Spiralling Parry and Punch, Withdraw and Push* and *Cross Hands*.Write down any personal insights in your journal.

3. Jot down three things you did when you saw yourself as a leader or sharing a leadership role (even if they were small roles).

4. Contemplate the Laws of Multiplication and Division of goods and services. See if you can identify three business companies that are multiplying their profits and redistributing their good fortune to help people, and another three business companies that are not doing this.

Part Two

To the Mountain:

'The Journey to Find the True Self'

Your palms gradually gather chi from the earth. Chi accumulates naturally in your tan-tien.

As chi energy is absorbed and begins to multiply, your chi sinks and opens up to limitless, loving chi. This beautiful chi naturally divides itself and shines like fields of radiant flowers in the sun, whose seeds are scattered in the wind.

These successes attract challenges and obstacles. You have the courage and stillness of the tiger and the mountain. You are caught up in the dance of ecstatic union of Yin/feminine and Yang/masculine attributes. Indescribable peace pervades your belly.

A sense of timelessness is all around. Let go. Feel empty and expansive. Chi gathers and brings together the opposite parts in you. You feel separate and yet as one.

The secrets of the Five Elements of Nature are in your hands. You stand like a tree with roots penetrating the earth and fruits celebrating the sky. Another aspect of you sinks down through your tan-tien and feet into the ground. When problems rush at you like a hurricane, you know how to yield and transform resistance into assistance.

You channel the reactive forces into creative pursuits.

From the stillness, you withdraw, and feel as if you are in the centre of a whirlwind.

A gentle presence of harmonious chi embraces the highest and lowest selves within you. As the grandparent becomes like a child, the child shall grow to be as the grandparent one day. Each helps each other to be wiser and more accepting of the other, one little step at a time. You step back to see your whole life harmoniously evolving, slowly and naturally. Free your ambitious side to pursue your highest aspirations, but at the same time let the householder part of you keep you always grounded so that you will be able to bring your inspirations back to earth and share in the treasure you have discovered.

Flow with your Yin and Yang polarities, like clouds falling as rain, evaporating to form playful clouds again.

Chi from your tan-tien exchanges chi with your heart centre.

CHAPTER SIX

Stand Like a Tree Rooted into the Mountain and Flowers Opening to the Sky

POSTURE 17

Embrace Tiger Return to Mountain

These successes attract challenges and obstacles. You have the courage and stillness of the tiger and the mountain.

1. Take a step with your right foot towards the south-east. From here, shift 70% of your weight on to your right foot. Move your left foot in to face 45 degrees south-east, turning from your waist. Move the right palm upward to face forward. Stretch your left hand, palm down, to the right (south-east), and look directly over it **(A, B)**.

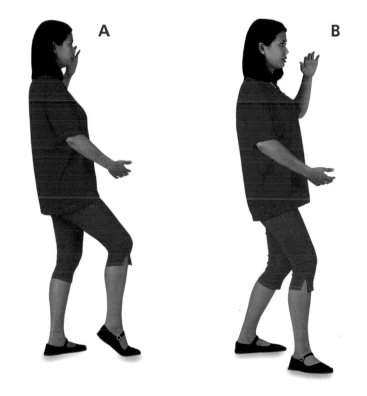

POSTURES 17A, B AND C

This sequence is a repetition of postures 5–7 of *Grasp the Sparrow's Tail, Press and Push – Rollback* (see pp. 31-34), but done facing south-east rather than east.

You are caught in the dance of ecstatic union of Yin/feminine and Yang/masculine attributes. Indescribable peace pervades your belly. A sense of timelessness is all around. Let go. Feel empty and expansive. Chi gathers and brings together the opposite parts in you. You feel separate and yet as one.

POSTURES 17D

This step is a repetition of Posture 8, *Single Whip* (see pp. 36-38), but done facing north-west rather than west.

The True Self

Many spiritual teachings embrace the idea that we exist in a dualistic relationship between our lower and higher selves. For centuries, this has been seen as a relationship of conflict, usually resolved by the submission of the lower self.

The Tai-Chi story is different. In *Embrace Tiger/Return to Mountain*, the conflict between the higher and lower selves can be resolved by embracing challenges and obstacles, and finding appropriate responses from a stance based on stillness in motion. *Grasp the Sparrow's Tail* teaches the lower and higher selves to harmonize with each other in a dance. In the *Step Back and Play with Monkey* sequence, the higher and lower selves mirror each other and discover that the two aspects are interchangeable.

I saw this in action when I visited Hua Shan, the Chinese Taoist mountain, a place of pilgrimage for thousands of Chinese. The journey was fraught with difficulties, and on five separate occasions my guide, a Tai-Chi Master, had to deal with drivers who demanded more money, or suddenly decided they didn't want to go to the mountain at all! But he managed to get us to our destination by cleverly embracing all the obstacles and harmonizing the Yin and Yang of the situation without any show of aggression.

A Journey Back to Her True Self

Pamela had recently realized that although she had been practising her T'ai-Chi resolutely and had benefited a lot from it, her mind had been restless. I showed her how to allow the mind to be restless but at the same time learn to meditate with the help of Nature. Pamela bought a plant, which became a friend to her, and helped her become much more relaxed. Her mind was still restless, however.

The mind is like a film director sitting in a series of inner cinemas, continuously watching films and editing some of them in the process. This director is the thinker, the observer who believes he is different from his film and its actors. He controls everything behind the scenes. But is he any different from the characters he has invented in his mind? Is it possible in daily life that this 'observer' also exists and believes itself to be the 'real' self, making judgements, comments, etc? Is it the 'real self'? The mind does not know how to establish its own limits. It can do all sorts of wonderful things, but this 'doer' is as unreal as all that it creates. Every thought is changeable and transient. This is not the real self.

I went to the cinema the other day and at the end of the film, people in the audience stood and applauded. I was amazed. There was no live performer to hear them. The audience had become so absorbed in the film that they forgot it was all just pictures on a white screen. I could see faces in the audience crying, getting angry, laughing and screaming with horror at different points in the film as if every thought and feeling out there on the screen and in their mind was real. Does life exist beyond the inner cinemas of the mind?

Pamela didn't understand what she could do about all this. But this 'doer' is precisely the issue, isn't it? When it is questioning, it thinks about how to stop all this restless thought and feeling, and at the same time, it is aware that it is, in itself, the problem. But when the mind understands its own limitations, it will naturally and effortlessly stop. Pamela felt deeply peaceful.

The next step is to become aware also of how the chi is moving around the heart area of the body. Pamela felt subtle movements of spiralling energies flowing through her whole being and bringing her into a strange space where the mind did not understand what it was. She found her consciousness expansive and enlivened. We then went out into the beautiful open spaces around the school and did T'ai-Chi. She felt the spaces in between herself and the trees and hills, and melted into a deep inner peace. She had begun her journey with her real self to her inner Mountain of Peace.

POSTURE 18

The Spiralling Punch Under the Elbow

When in confusion and turmoil, let go and withdraw and return to your breath and spiralling chi and rest there in tranquillity.

1. Draw back from the *Single Whip* position and shift most of your weight on to your right foot **(A)**.

A

B

C

2. Withdraw both arms simultaneously towards your abdomen, shift your weight on to the left foot and slide your right foot to the back of your left heel **(B, C)**.

3. Turn from your waist and allow both arms to turn like a wheel slowly around your waist. The right palm turns to the back and circles round, followed by the right hand, gliding to the left side of your waist **(D, E, F)**.

D

E

F

Please note carefully the way the thumb and fingers open (traditionally known as the 'Tiger's Mouth') to receive the left palm **(G, H)**.

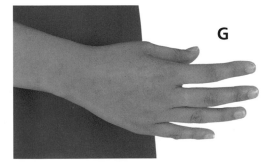

G

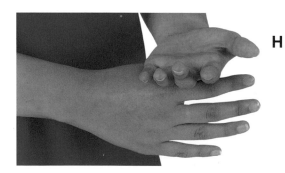

H

4. The right foot steps forward at 45 degrees, and your weight shifts forward on to your right leg **(I)**. Your right thumb and first finger form a little circle, which will receive the left elbow **(J)**. Glide the left palm across the little circular formation. You are facing north-west **(K, L)**.

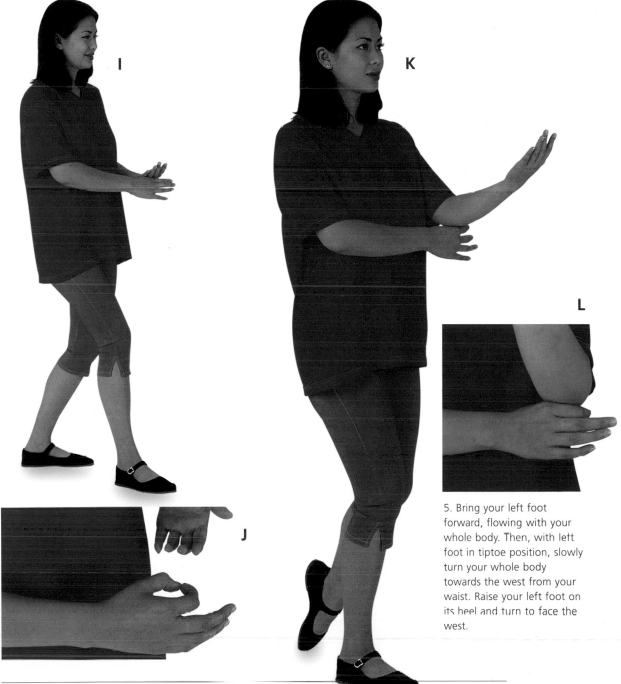

5. Bring your left foot forward, flowing with your whole body. Then, with left foot in tiptoe position, slowly turn your whole body towards the west from your waist. Raise your left foot on its heel and turn to face the west.

SPIRALLING BREATH

The purpose of this guided meditation is to help you discover a more energizing way to breathe. This exercise will particularly benefit people who have breathing difficulties such as asthmatics, as well as those who feel they are generally lacking in stamina.

Imagine a clock on your lap. See its clockwise motion. Breathe in slowly.

If you can reach a count from one to seven, that would be best.

Imagine your breath like smoke spiralling upwards, in a clockwise direction.

Let your lungs and tan-tien fill up. Pause.

Breathe out. Observe the anti-clockwise direction. Let your lungs and tan-tien deflate.

See your breath like smoke spiralling downwards.

Count up to seven.

How to Allow Chi to Energize You

By this stage of T'ai-Chi learning, you will have experienced something of the benefit and value of chi. The next step is to explore the way in which chi is limitlessly inside and around us all the time.

The mental cessation of 'trying' The way of chi in nature is 'effortless effort'. Any attempt you make to understand this is in itself an effort, which therefore moves away from the limitless nature of chi. When people look at me to try to understand what I am talking about, this mental effort is based on the assumption that they do not already understand what I am trying to share with them. If chi is limitless, it must be in you already, right now.

A student recently asked me whether chi was the stillness experienced in meditation, adding that when we are still, the chi is flowing. The answer is yes – for beginners, this may be a very important stage in the recognition of chi.

In the next step, however, we would like to encourage the mind to comprehend how every attempt to understand limitlessness in chi is futile. The mind cannot touch that which is beyond itself, just as a computer cannot understand that which is beyond its mechanism. No matter how rational and realistic a program it comes up with, it can only operate within its perimeters. So, when the mind understands that 'stillness meditation' is also about 'trying', it recognizes that 'trying' is not effortless effort.

The emotional experience of 'effortless effort' Look at Nature. Have you ever noticed a tree grow day by day, week by week, month by month, year by year? I urge you to obtain a bonsai tree for your home. Sit silently with the tree. Do not expect feel much at first. Just learn to take care of it, and be with it. This tree will one day be your friend and teach you about effortless effort. Every tiny bit of relaxation in your body is rooting you deeper into a natural awareness that chi is already in you.

Learn to trust chi with your whole being Your trust in chi is something that comes to you in infinite degrees. By now, you may already be starting to feel it flowing, sometimes in your fingers, wrists, legs or back, or sometimes even through your whole body. What would you do if you were really very tired and aching all over? Would you sit down and trust the chi to energize you? Your hunched shoulders can learn to trust chi more by relaxing, loosening up and allowing the whole body to 'Be Held' by chi. Chi is physically all around you.

Spiritually, open up to allow chi to flow into your blood vessels It is when chi flows through your blood vessels and frees up your whole body, internally, that natural health and harmony permeate. This helps prevent illnesses and imbalances from occurring in your immune system. In contrast to spiritual practices that require you to adopt the philosophies of a master or to surrender your self to a spiritual energy outside yourself, here you let yourself 'Be Held' by chi in your heart, body, mind and spirit.

So, it is this energizing experience that makes you realize that chi is already inside your body! (For a deeper experience of this, using your breath, see p. 162.)

The last stage comes when you realize that chi is intelligent.

It already knows where your areas of bodily imbalance are. Let it adjust the Yin and Yang levels without you needing to do anything. Relax into the silent, growing process... you are growing in chi as you are, right now.

HOMEWORK 6

1. Practise *Embrace Tiger/Return to Mountain* sequence (in a fixed position for 15 minutes) and then sit down while you meditate on the stillness of mountains. It may help to recollect something in your past that is connected with mountains, or alternatively bring to mind any pictures of mountains that have particularly impressed you in some way.

2. Learn how to breathe in a spiral pattern with your in-breath and out-breath.

3. Practise the *Spiralling Punch Under the Elbow*, slowly, and feel your tan-tien guiding every single step you make. And then, again. Practise this for 10 minutes. This exercise will help you learn how to harmonize with chi in your breathing. It uses the same method the ancient Taoists used when they learned to breathe through their feet and thereby promote longevity and good health.

CHAPTER SEVEN
Celebrate Who You Truly Are, Right Now

POSTURE 19
Step Back and Play with Monkey, Right Side

A gentle presence of harmonious chi embraces the highest and lowest selves within you. As the grandparent becomes like a child, the child shall grow to be like a grandparent one day. Each is helping each other to be wiser and more accepting of the other, one little step at a time. You step back to see your whole life harmoniously evolving, slowly and naturally.

1. Rest your left elbow on the circle formed by your right thumb and forefinger. Open your right hand and draw it back, palm up, to your right ear. Turn the palm down. At the same time extend and sink your left hand out in front of you. Now the left palm is facing up, towards the right palm that is facing down. It is as if they mirror each other **(A, B)**.

2. Step back lightly with your left foot and put it down toes first, so that it points straight ahead (west). Shift your weight on to your left foot and turn your right toes inward so that your feet are parallel. Bring your right palm past your right ear, thrust it directly forward and then let it sink down in front of the tan-tien **(C)**.

3. Your right palm now faces upwards in the direction of your left palm. At the same time, circle backwards with your left hand, palm up, and bring it back to your left ear **(D)**.

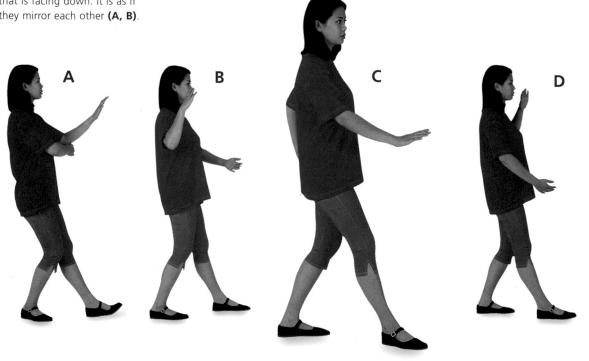

A   B   C   D

POSTURE **20**B

Step Back and Play with Monkey, Left Side

Your right palm, positioned near your tan-tien, is facing upwards, and your left palm is beside your left ear, facing down. It is as if they mirror each other. Step lightly back with your right foot and put it down, toes first, so that it points straight ahead (west). Shift your weight on to your right foot and turn your right toes inward so that your feet are parallel. Bring your right palm past your right ear. At the same time, bring your left hand, palm facing upwards, back to your left side in front of your tan-tien **(A)**.

POSTURE **20**B

Step Back and Play with Monkey, Right Side

This is a repetition of Posture 19 (see opposite).

Start from the position in which your left palm is facing up towards your right palm, which is facing down. It is as if they mirror each other. Step lightly back with your left foot and place it down toes first, so that it points straight ahead (west). Shift your weight on to your left foot and turn your right toes in so that your feet are parallel. Bring your right palm past your right ear, thrust it directly forward and let it sink down in front of your tan-tien. Your right palm now faces upwards, towards your left palm.

At the same time, circle backwards with your left hand, palm up, and bring it back to your left side, beside your left ear.

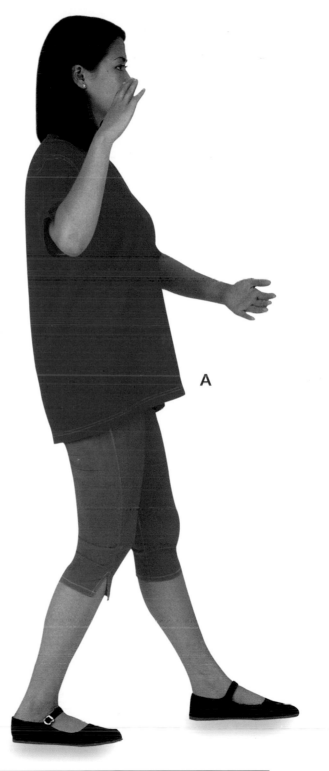

A

THE FLOWERING OF HUMANITY

For deepening your practice and appreciation of the *Step Back and Play with Monkey* sequence, go through the following practical meditation exercise.

Get an indoor flowering bulb. Plant it with love and gentleness. Have it quite close by you, by your bedside. Take care of it every day, watering it but not overdoing it.

When you see the first signs of something coming out of the soil, sit with it for about 10 minutes.

When you see the flower, sit with it longer – about 15-30 minutes.

Go through the exercises described on page 74 on
How to Allow Chi to Energise You.

When you can feel the chi flowing effortlessly in you, do this exercise. Very slowly and gradually stretch out your hand and feel chi connecting you to the flower. Then move your hand back towards your heart and receive the chi from the flower. The good feelings you feel help the flowering of goodness and kindness in your humanity.

Do this about 10 times every day for two weeks.

Instead of just feeling the chi between you and the flower, I would like you to touch and caress a petal of the flower with chi. Stroke it with utmost tenderness, as if you are touching the soft cheeks of a baby's face.

Can you feel the chi flowing? Feeling the chi flowering down to its roots, too.

You will have a richer and deeper appreciation when you recommence your
Step Back and Play with Monkey.

POSTURE 21

Diagonal Flying

Free your ambitious side to pursue your highest aspirations, but at the same time let the householder part of you keep you always grounded so that you will be able to bring your inspirations back to earth and share in the treasure you have discovered.

From rose red, blue takes over naturally once more, and inspires the dancer to attain new heights of creativity.

1. From the *Step Back and Play with Monkey* posture, bring your left hand around to the front, level with your head, and rest your right hand beside your tan-tien. All your weight is concentrated on your left foot **(A)**.

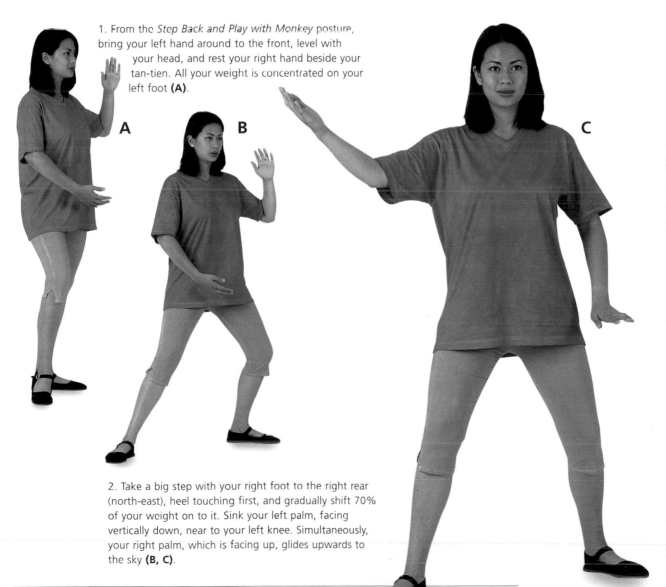

A **B** **C**

2. Take a big step with your right foot to the right rear (north-east), heel touching first, and gradually shift 70% of your weight on to it. Sink your left palm, facing vertically down, near to your left knee. Simultaneously, your right palm, which is facing up, glides upwards to the sky **(B, C)**.

DIAGONAL FLYING

When the left palm/Yin side sinks down and the right palm/Yang side diagonally floats up, two aspects clearly emerge. The left, Yin side is like the homemaker, while the right Yang side is like the ambitious partner who goes out to work to earn more money for the home. Is there a space where these two aspects can come together to learn to flow with each other?

Sometimes, these two personalities may find it difficult to flow with each other harmoniously. The homemaker may feel envious of the breadwinner, while he or she in turn may wish for more time at home. Naturally, this can cause a lot of tension and resentment. However, when you accept that you have both of these aspects inside you, and you see how they are both equally important in your daily life, your attitude changes. The householder part of you values the time it has to let go, relax and create a homely atmosphere, while the ambitious part of you is allowed the excitement of challenges and the luxury of intellectual and inspirational space.

This is what T'ai-Chi does. It draws the Yin and Yang within you into a more harmonious relationship.

You can also sit down and practise it the other way round, as well. First the left palm is facing downwards and sinks to the earth while the right palm is flying off at a tangent to the upper right. Now, you reverse it. The left palm is flying off at a tangent to the upper left, and the right palm is facing downwards and sinks to the earth. And then you can swap over again.

Another purpose of this exercise is to help you discover that the Yin is present in the Yang principles, and the Yang is in the Yin principles, too. This means that the homemaker can experience household work as an art form in itself, and with such a creative attitude may uncover an incredible wealth of inspiration and drive that will ensure success in an ambitious way. The ambitious worker may in turn discover a new depth of peace and a great reservoir of wisdom by slowing down to become simple and totally present at home.

POSTURE 22
Wave Hands in Clouds, Right

Flow with your Yin and Yang polarities, like clouds falling as rain, evaporating to form playful clouds again. Chi from your tan-tien exchanges chi with your heart centre. When you allow your whole being to be as soft and ever-changing as the clouds, your physical movements will naturally follow.

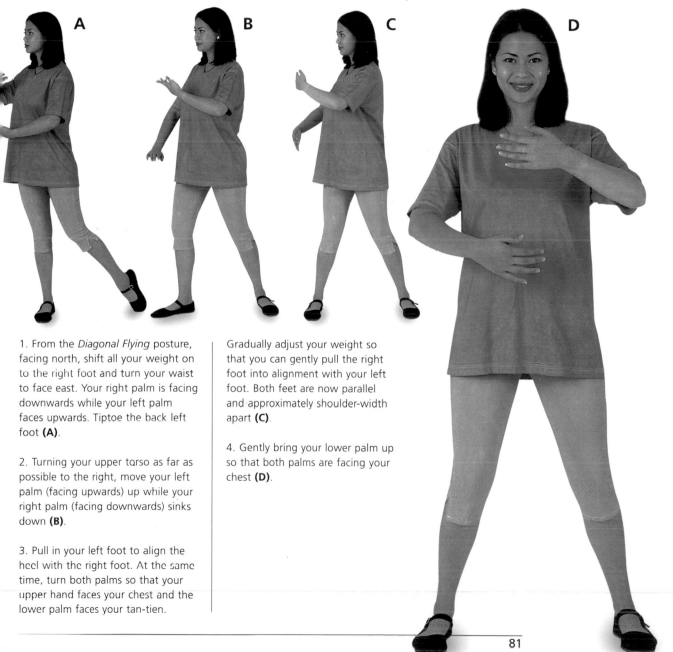

1. From the *Diagonal Flying* posture, facing north, shift all your weight on to the right foot and turn your waist to face east. Your right palm is facing downwards while your left palm faces upwards. Tiptoe the back left foot **(A)**.

2. Turning your upper torso as far as possible to the right, move your left palm (facing upwards) up while your right palm (facing downwards) sinks down **(B)**.

3. Pull in your left foot to align the heel with the right foot. At the same time, turn both palms so that your upper hand faces your chest and the lower palm faces your tan-tien.

Gradually adjust your weight so that you can gently pull the right foot into alignment with your left foot. Both feet are now parallel and approximately shoulder-width apart **(C)**.

4. Gently bring your lower palm up so that both palms are facing your chest **(D)**.

POSTURE 23A
Wave Hands in Clouds, Left

1. Turn your body to face west. Gradually shift your weight on to your left foot and raise your right foot slightly to bring it half a shoulder-width closer to the left foot **(A)**. Simultaneously, the right palm goes up and the left palm sinks down.

2. Turn your body to face north again **(B)**.

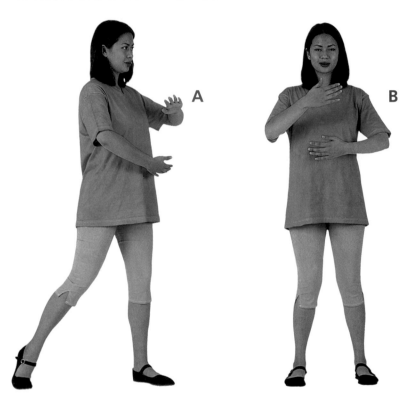

POSTURE 23B
Wave Hands in Clouds, Right

1. Continuing from Posture 23A, turn your body towards the east again and repeat (as shown in **A** and **B** on page 81). As you turn from your waist towards the right, raise the left foot slightly and take a small step back, so that both feet are now back to normal shoulder-width position. Your left palm comes up and the right palm sink downs.

2. As you do this last movement, shift some weight to the right foot and raise your left foot to take a half step so that your feet are now wider apart (the width of your shoulders).

3. Both arms are held as if you are hugging a tree. Slowly turn the upper half of your body towards the left side until you are facing north (as shown in **A**, above).

DANCE WITH THE CLOUDS

Relax your palms in front of you and feel as if your hands are truly in the clouds;

Your palms are holding a fluffy ball of cloud in between them.

Turn the ball around you and feel the spaces filled with billions of dots of chi energy.

Let your mind melt into this space... this space is you, right now.

You are a ball of chi energy gently floating around your body.

Relax your arms, elbows and wrists as if they are supported by cotton wool

And feel as if you are a cloud, moving slowly... changing shape, size

and texture all the time.

Keep relaxing your mind;

All your thoughts are also made of chi energy.

Keep concentrating on the spaces between your palms –

You feel freer and freer, and so expansive.

You are disappearing... all that remains is this sense of tingling energy

around you. You are in a gaseous state. Your hands and whole body are tingling, all over,

right now.

Your arms are freely flowing in clouds of energy;

You are free.

Your mind is free and empty

Your heart feels full and released

Gently, now, bring both palms together and place one palm on your chest

and the other on your stomach.

Be still,

quiet

feel that lovely, spacious silence still here... now

And now, bringing both palms in front of your chest in the position of prayer,

feel grateful and respectful to chi.

HOMEWORK 7

1. Practise the following sequences - *Step Back and Play with Monkey, Diagonal Flying* and *Wave Hands in Clouds*. Write down your insights about this section in relation to how your body is assimilating the exercises – the wrists, elbows and belly-centre co-ordination with the legs.

2. In what way do the following sequences help you understand how to know yourself better?
   a. The *Step Back and Play with Monkey* sequence. Can you think of some examples of these dual higher and lower selves in conflict or in harmonious interaction, either in yourself or in friends or relatives?
   b. The *Diagonal Flying* sequence. Which aspect do you think needs further development in yourself – the householder or the ambitious side of you?
   c. The *Wave Hands in Clouds* sequence. Name some hobbies or interests that you think enable you to 'let go completely and disappear into timeless joy'.

Part Three

Heaven, Humanity and Earth:

'Finding the Circle of Life'

As you are gradually sinking back down into the earth, feel chi rising up to nourish your body. Heavenly Chi, Human Chi and Earth Chi flow in your body movements all the time.

You are centred as a tree, rooting, growing, flowing and flowering. Humbling yourself, you spiral into the earth and allow abundant Earth Chi to spiral back to you, flowing through the centre of your tan-tien, heart and head. Chi circulates up your spine and down your front. Abundant, prosperous, creative energy explodes from the centre of your being and is shared spontaneously with the world around you. As you turn within and find the union of your inner mother, father and child principles, they help you achieve balance and creative strength. Affirm your goals and consistently hold them clear in your vision, and you will get there promptly. Stepping forward to claim what is rightfully yours, you humble yourself to the Earth Spirit and take heed from the wisdom of the Five Elements. This natural knowledge helps you control the dual forces in your daily life. Conflicting situations transform into a circular dance of Yin and Yang. Their only purpose is to find the point of union, and let go into infinite expansive space again. From nothingness comes the spontaneous, creative spark. As it reaches its climax, it, too, is released and excess energy is gathered. Sink back into a quiet, peaceful and happy place. You are like a tree finding its rightful place in the soil.

CHAPTER EIGHT
The Path of Self-knowledge Is Circular

POSTURE 23C
Wave Hands into Single Whip/ Snake Creeps Down

Heavenly Chi, Human Chi and Earth Chi flow in your body movements all the time.

As with every high, there is a downward spiral, and thus the journey into the Snake Creeps Down sequence is a journey into the power of red, the colour of the rich earth. Golden Cock Stands On One Leg exemplifies the circulation of creative energy from the earth to the sky and through the body of the dancer.

1. From the final stage of *Wave Hands*, facing north, turn your waist towards the left and shift your weight slightly on to your right foot. Shift the weight on the left foot on to the heel and turn with the waist. Let both arms follow the swing of the waist to the left, left palm facing up, right palm facing down. At the same time, turn your left foot 45 degrees to the left (**A, B**).

2. Gently shift your weight on to the left foot and raise your right foot to step forward. Both palms follow the forward movement, left palm facing up and right palm facing down. Lift up both arms up to shoulder height (**C, D, E**).

3. With all your weight anchored on the right foot, tiptoe the left foot and prepare to take a step with your left foot, in a westerly direction.

The left foot and left arm move gently to the left side, the left palm facing you and the right palm facing down. As you sink down, turn the left palm out while your right-hand fingers collect into a bird's beak formation.

Feel rooted like a tree. The left palm (Yin) is as open as the leaves and flowers, and the right fingers (Yang) are held tightly, as rigid and penetrating as the roots themselves (**F, G, H**).

POSTURE 24
Squatting Single Whip

You are centred as a tree, rooting, growing, flowing and flowering. Humbling yourself, you spiral into the earth and allow abundant earth chi to spiral back to you.

1. Turn your right foot on its heel to the right as you draw back and lower your body, so that you are squatting over your right foot **(A, B)**.

A

B

C

D

E

2. Simultaneously, draw your left arm inward, back to your right thigh. Sink and describe a downward arc with your left hand along your left leg and lean forward as you turn on your left heel 45 degrees to the left. Your right hand remains in a bird-beak formation. Your left hand rests above the left knee **(C, D, E)**.

POSTURE 25

Golden Cock Stands on One Leg, Right

When the chi circulates through your body, you can slow it down. In this way, you can experience the small circulation of chi that goes up your spine and comes down through the front of your body.

1. As you thrust your left hand forward **(A)**, turn your right foot on its heel 45 degrees towards the left, bend your left knee slightly, and shift weight on to it. Your right-hand fingers relax from the bird-beak formation **(B)**.

2. Turn your left foot 45 degrees towards the left as you begin to rise **(C)**. Raise your right hand, drawing it up from between your thighs **(D)**. You are facing south-west **(E)**.

3. Turn to face west **(F)**. Standing on your bent left leg, raise your right leg, knee bent, so that your toes point downwards. Raise your right arm and hold it vertically above your knee. Your left arm sinks down. Your right-hand movement is closer to your chest than your left arm movement. Leave your left hand between your thighs, the elbow slightly bent **(G)**.

F

G

POSTURE 26

Golden Cock Stands on One Leg, Left

1. Gently put your right foot down one step behind you, moving
45 degrees behind the left ankle **(A)**. Allow your toes to touch the
floor first. Turn the left foot on its heel so that your feet are parallel
to each other **(B)**.

A

B

2. Slowly raise your left leg, knee bent, so that your toes point down **(C)**. At the same time, raise your left arm and hold it vertically above your knee. Your right hand remains between your thighs, the elbow slightly bent **(D, E)**.

C   **D**   **E**

POSTURE 27

Separate Right Foot, the Sunburst Kick

Your upper and lower limbs join together in your tan-tien to release the chi in one fast movement. Abundant, prosperous, creative energy explodes from the centre of your being and is shared spontaneously with the world around you.

Balancing this red energy is the yellow sequence of the Sunburst Kick, *the inner spark that comes alight when you allow Yin, Yang and Tao to come together naturally and effortlessly.*

1. Slowly put your left foot down to the left rear, about 45 degrees behind your right heel, and shift your weight on to it **(A)**.

2. Turn your right foot on its heel so that it is parallel to the left foot **(B)**.

3. Keep your left arm still. Then, raise your right palm so that it brushes under the left lower arm and palm **(C)**.

A

B

C

D

4. Open and stretch both arms from your elbows and time the rhythm of your arm movements with the kick of the right foot from the knee **(D)**.

This movement is done slowly at first and then faster when you feel more confident. The movement comes from the torso.

POSTURE **28**
Separate Left Foot

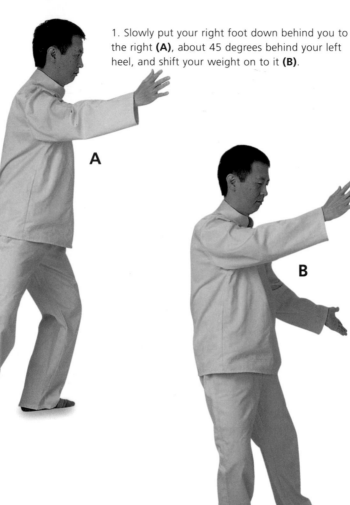

1. Slowly put your right foot down behind you to the right **(A)**, about 45 degrees behind your left heel, and shift your weight on to it **(B)**.

2. Turn your left foot on its heel so that it is parallel to the right foot. Your arms naturally follow the waist and feet. Keep your right arm still. Then, raise your left palm so that it brushes under the right arm and palm **(C)**.

3. Open and stretch both arms from your elbows and at the same time raise your left leg (D). Time the rhythm of your arm movements with the kick of the left foot from the knee (E). This movement is done slowly at first and then faster when you feel more confident. The movement comes from the torso.

D

E

HOMEWORK 8

1. Practise the following sequences: *Squatting Single Whip/Snake Creeps Down*, *Golden Cock Stands on One Leg* and *Sunburst Kick*. Jot down any personal insights you have into the movements.

2. In *Snake Creeps Down*, describe how the Earth Chi connects to your movements.

3. When you do *Golden Cock Stands on One Leg*, learn to stand on one leg with your eyes closed. This will improve your balance.

4. Do the *Sunburst Kick* more and more slowly. When you do it slowly, you can use the slowness to learn how to co-ordinate your movements from your tan-tien. Then, gradually increase the speed as you get more confident standing on one leg.

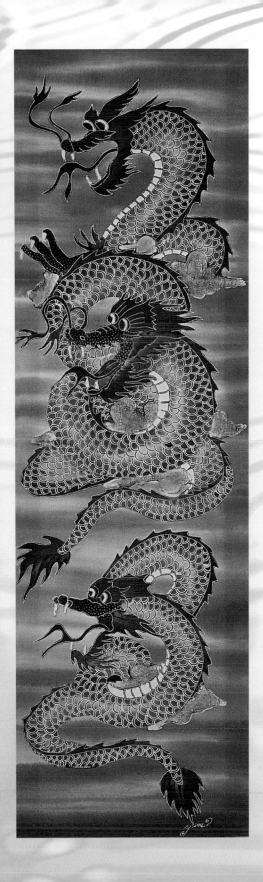

Part Four

Happiness in Service:

'Fulfilment'

The final part of the Rainbow T'ai-Chi Form reveals the indigo qualities of leadership and selfless service with the Greeting the Seven Stars sequence, completing the Rainbow T'ai-Chi Dance in a spirit of unity in diversity.

Sinking into the tan-tien centre, you turn to face four ways in which you can know yourself and serve the world. Spiralling and interweaving energy brings you to meet the north-east, the path of Lightning and Thunder. You learn how to achieve synthesis, and help yourself and others go beyond the dimension of duality. Joy and humour are your friends. In the north-west, you return to the Mountain within you and find infinite peace.

Allow the world to come to you. You have done enough and you rest in the stillness. In the south-west, you ride on the Wind and flow with whatever destiny brings you. You humble yourself and respect the whole earth as your home. In the south-east, you return to the Lake and see every experience in your daily life as a reflection of your true self. In your open heart, you hear the courtships of animals and of humankind as blissful dances of Yin and Yang. You watch with compassion the search of Yang by Yin and Yin by Yang. The yearning of both to find the creative union, the Tao. And then, there is the discovery of Wu-Chi, the great Nothingness. From nothingness, fresh and revitalizing ideas are born.

From the rebirth of new energy, your roots go beyond this earth as you spiral down to the other side and find the Seven Stars, your seven rainbow qualities. You have an open invitation to rise and join them, become as a star shining, multiplying the chi in you, limitless universal energy encircling you and the earth. The radiant power of chi shines in all that you do. Your goals are realized right now. You awaken to who you really are. As the spiral of life continues, every day is an opportunity to gather the precious energy from the Five Elements and learn the wisdom of Nature. You learn to let go, to trust the chi energy and fulfil your destiny, right now.

There are many ways to serve with your heart, body, mind and spirit.

In Fair Lady Works at Shuttles, the north-easterly movement demonstrates that you do not need to be that heavy and serious when you are learning how to help yourself and others go beyond duality and achieve synthesis. Recently I was in a crowded tube train that had stopped in a tunnel. Over the loud speaker came a voice that sounded like an impersonation of Marilyn Monroe confessing that no one knew how long we would have to wait there. Passengers were irritable and frustrated. A tall man crammed in next to me was eating a large sandwich, which had an aroma that would tantalize anyone! And he was holding this delicious masterpiece right in front of my face. I said, 'If you get any closer, your sandwich will be in my mouth, and you will have to ask for a refund for that, too!' He laughed, and actually asked me if I would like to have a bite. Other people started laughing as well, and the atmosphere in the carriage quickly became friendlier and lighter. (And no, I did not take a bite of his sandwich!)

In the north-westerly direction, Fair Lady Works at Shuttles shows you a peaceful way to serve, and to wait and see just what your effort brings. I have a very heart-centred (and hard-working) student who has been practising chi healing. She built up her own reservoirs of stillness and patience by working with a few people, and those she helped recommended her to others. Very soon she was practising with many more people. Whatever you are learning, it is always good to take it slowly, a few steps at a time.

In the south-westerly direction, you learn to flow with whatever comes your way and humbly serve, wherever you are. Recently, another student came to work with me. She was confused about where she should live, work and put down roots. After practising T'ai-Chi heartbeat listening and working with these issues, she realized she had to restart her T'ai-Chi classes in a new hall where she felt happy. Because she put her whole heart, body, mind and spirit into finding a new place to live, she became a magnet for new possibilities. Often, people think they should settle in one place and not uproot themselves. In some cases that may be true, but people are not trees! The planet is our place of service; wherever we go, we can serve.

The south-easterly direction of Fair Lady Works at Shuttles highlights the connection between serving outside and serving inside. It is about choice, too. You can choose to see or not to see reflections of your true self in the Yin/Yang courtship dance. I was in the park the other day, feeding the squirrels and birds, and observing their courtship rituals, a unique celebration of Yin and Yang. There were couples walking through the park. Some were so absorbed in their relationship that they didn't notice the squirrels at all. Others experienced so much joy sharing their love with the animals that the animals responded with gratitude not just for the food but also for the loving chi radiated out to them.

Many T'ai-Chi groups choose to work mainly at one level. For example, recently a very experienced T'ai-Chi teacher remarked that he could not understand why we were interested in the application of T'ai-Chi principles in everyday life, which was a subject he thought was best left to sociologists. But if T'ai-Chi comes from Nature and if Humanity is the beneficiary of its ancient wisdom and richness, where else can we find it but in human interaction? The body language of two people who are truly flowing with each other will manifest the movements of the Yin and Yang dance whether they know it consciously or not. The ancient T'ai-Chi and Taoist Masters have always insisted that the Laws of Yin and Yang are universal and found in every part of our lives. People who choose to separate their activities into little compartments may forget that all the rooms are part of one beautiful mansion.

It is with this holistic vision of sharing the T'ai-Chi message with the world that we find ourselves manifesting what we believe in. We love to help people grow. We are excited when we see people finding their way home to their chi-energizing selves. They are learning how to be nourished by chi and lead a happier and more fulfilled life.

Growing and Sharing Food with the Homeless

For the past thirty years, my students and I have practised Tai-Chi in co-operation with the elements of nature. The chi energy we have been growing has now come full circle, for we have been putting our energies into growing fruit and vegetables, planted in a circular formation, in our school grounds. People have practised Tai-Chi amongst the trees and potimarron plants.

Potimarron plants yield nutritious fruits – like a cross between a chestnut and pumpkin – that grow to the size of a football. They are not only delicious but also have medicinal properties recognized by Japanese doctors. They can be kept fresh if the stem is kept dry. Last year we managed to produce enough to enable us to give hundreds of them to soup kitchens serving homeless people. They were very appreciative of fresh, organic produce, which is normally so expensive, and took more than they needed so that they could freeze them for later use. Next year, we will try to expand our farming activities and grow even more vegetables.

When you share food with the homeless, you are really feeding a part of yourself – the humanity in you. There is a homeless part in each one of us.

On the physical level, we are not only concerned with the kind of loving and healthy chi energy we need to generate and channel into our internal organs, but we also extend our concern to the food we eat. Sharing enriching energy with the world is one way in which we can create Happiness in Service.

CHAPTER NINE

Serve With All Your Heart, Body, Mind and Spirit

POSTURE 29A

Turn and Strike with the Heel

Turn within to find the union with your inner mother, father and child principles; they help you achieve balance and creative strength. When this is applied at a group level, it is sometimes called the 'spontaneous chi combustion effect' (SCCE). This can produce instant chi-healing experiences.

The Sponaneous Chi Combustion Effect

There are many kinds of energy experiences people undergo when practising T'ai-Chi. In martial arts, chi is sometimes concentrated and channelled into the parts of the body where it can be used as an effective projection of force. Over the years I have had many martial arts students come to our classes for healing. Emphasis in our classes falls on health and rejuvenation, so we accumulate the chi for that purpose. When the group energy is very strong we sometimes practise group chi healing, and have conducted many such experiments over the past twenty years with success.

In the summer of 2000, for example, we conducted a simple experiment. From a group of just over twenty people gathered in a hall, two (A and B) who needed healing, accompanied by two others who were to record the patients' descriptions of the healing process, went to another building a short distance away. There they were separated, one downstairs and one upstairs. The group was divided into two smaller groups, which were requested not to project any energy to the patients, but instead to be aware of their own bodies; as chi is universal, their own chi was already connected to A and B. They were given simple movements to perform. An hour later, A and B, who did not know what the group was doing, reported experiencing remarkable energy! Light, colour, warmth, and tingling and a powerful healing sensation were affecting various parts of their body.

These chi healing sessions take place only when the energy of the group has reached a certain 'peak'; that is, when there is a dimension of pure chi available for everyone to tap into.

The Trilogue Experience

About 15 years ago, my T'ai-Chi and chi healing work connected at an emotional and mental level for the first time, through an exploration of the way we communicate. A monologue is like a lecture, and the audience is on the receiving end; at an inner level, one part of you lectures the other part. Then, there is the dualistic approach – a dialogue – where two sides discuss opposing views in a debate. But this may lead to a third possible way of understanding a problem.

This is a relatively new concept in the West, but in T'ai-Chi we have been concentrating on this Third Way for thousands of years. Learning how to conduct an inner trilogue is quite challenging if one has not first of all learned to establish the inner family of child,

mother and father principles. In the West, the child has been accorded a position of prime importance for many years.

It is only recently that greater emphasis has been placed on the adult understanding of the art of parenting and the art of teaching. In the Trilogue system, we place emphasis on the learning process that leads to understanding, and try to establish a fairer communication system between the inner family members. The inner mother, father and child should have equal opportunities to voice or express their opinions and feelings. Out of this sense of communion comes the opportunity to experience the fourth dimension, wherein true healing can take place.

A

1. Swing the right hand up towards the left and then down in a semicircle towards the right, to join the left hand. Raise your left foot off the ground. Retract your left foot to the back of the right heel **(A)**.

B

C

2. Shift some weight on to the front part of your left foot and turn your arms around 270 degrees **(B, C)**.

3. Keep your left arm still as the right arm circles round to cross at the lower left arm **(D)**. The right foot is pointing 45 degrees to the south and the left foot is tiptoeing, facing east. Both your arms are crossed **(E)**.

E

D

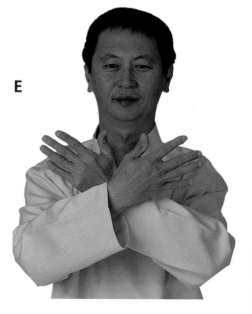

F

G

4. Slowly turn your arms from your waist **(F, G)**.

H

I

5. Raise your left knee to touch the left elbow and kick **(H, I)**. At the same time, the left arm makes a chopping motion with the fingers pointing up. This kick is different from Posture 28 in that the heel, rather than the toes, is used as the striking member and the kick is focused higher.

POSTURE 29B
Brush Left Knee and Twist Step

Affirm your goals, hold them constantly and clearly in your vision, and you will get there promptly.

A

1. From Position 29A (see p. 105), let your left foot sink down to a tiptoe position. Turn your left arm until the palm is just beside your left ear. You are facing east **(A)**.

B

2. Sink your left palm to the side of the left thigh, to brush your left knee. Let the left foot step forward into a square formation **(B, C)** and then sink your right hand down in the mid-point section directly in front of your chest, as in Posture 13C (see p. 54).

C

The T'ai-Chi Dance immediately flows into the violet energy of humbleness, healing and meekness, as the dancer steps forward and bends his head before the earth.

POSTURE 30

Turn Torso to Spiral Arms Towards the Right

1. Retract the weight of your body on to your right foot and swing both arms down gently towards the left side **(A)**.

2. Swing both your arms in a spiral forward direction. Shift your weight forward on to the left foot, turning your waist to co-ordinate the extension of your right foot forward **(B, C)**.

A

B

C

D

E

3. Put your right foot down pointing southeast and tiptoe your left foot **(D, E)**.

POSTURE 31A

Step Forward, Descend and Strike with Fist

Step forward to claim what is rightfully yours; you are deferential to the earth spirit and take heed from the wisdom of Nature's Five Elements.

1. Bring your left foot to the front **(A)** and extend it one square forward.

A

2. Bend down and sweep the left hand to brush past the left knee **(B)**.

B

3. Your right arm comes from the right side to punch downwards between the legs **(C)**.

C

POSTURE 31B
Grasp the Sparrow's Tail

Flow with the Yin/Yang aspects of each step you take.

1. Sink your weight on to your right foot and turn your arms from your torso towards the left **(A)**.

A

2. Swing your arms back into *Grasp the Sparrow's Tail, Ward-off, Right* **(B)**.

B

3. Move the arms from the torso, as in Posture 5, *Grasp the Sparrow's Tail*, Rollback (see p. 31) **(C)**.

C

4. Repeat
Posture 6,
*Grasp the
Sparrow's
Tail, Press*
(**D, E, F, G,
H, I,** see pp.
32-34).

D

E

F

G

H

I

6. Withdraw your weight on to your left foot, sinking both arms, in a parallel position, back towards the waist **(J)**. Turn your body, swing both arms to the west and bring them both back to hold a ball-shape. Take a step towards the west into the *Single Whip* position.

J

POSTURE 32

Fair Lady Works at Shuttles, Right to North-East

Chi energy guides you towards the north-east, the paths of Lightning and Thunder. You learn how to achieve synthesis, and help yourself and others go beyond the dimension of duality. Joy and humour are your friends.

The Fair Lady Works at Shuttles exudes the orange qualities of joy, vitality and lightness, which are the keys to the door to new vocational opportunities.

1. From the *Single Whip* position, facing west, withdraw your arms and the weight of your body towards the belly centre **(A)**.

A

2. Simultaneously shift your weight on to your right foot **(B)**. Turn your left foot inward as far as you can, towards the north-east **(C)**.

B

C

3. Keep some of your weight on the heel of your right foot and the rest on your left foot. Shift the weight on to your left foot and relax the tensed right foot so that it turns on its heel. Your left palm and right palm are turning with your waist.

5. Turn your right palm in a small circle and at the same time, take a step towards the north-east, placing your left foot in a north-easterly direction **(D)**.

D

E

6. Shift 70% of your weight on to your left foot. Lift up both arms from your torso to push up gently from your tan-tien, towards the north-east **(E, F)**.

F

POSTURE 32A

Fair Lady Works at Shuttles, Facing North-West

In this direction, you turn within and return to the Mountain within you to find infinite peace. All the world will come to you. You have done enough and you rest in stillness.

1. From the north-east, withdraw your right arm under your left arm. Sink the weight of your body on to your right foot **(A)**.

A

2. Raise your left foot slightly and turn it inwards as far as you can, towards the south **(B, C)**.

B   **C**

D

3. Keep most of your weight on the right foot. At the same time, bring your right palm under your left hand, towards your elbow **(D)**.

4. Shift all your weight on to your right foot. Allow the right palm to slide from under your left arm, so that both arms are now parallel to each other. Move your body slowly towards the north-west. Support the body while it turns by pivoting part of your weight on to the front of your right foot **(E)**.

E

F

5. Take a step with your right foot towards the north-west **(F)**.

G

6. Shift 70% of your weight on to your right foot and turn your left foot on its heel, 45 degrees. Simultaneously, move from the torso and shift your arms up into *Fair Lady Works at Shuttles*, facing north-west **(G)**.

POSTURE 32B

Fair Lady Works at Shuttles, Facing South-West

You ride upon the wind and flow with whatever Destiny brings you. You humble yourself and respect the whole earth as your home.

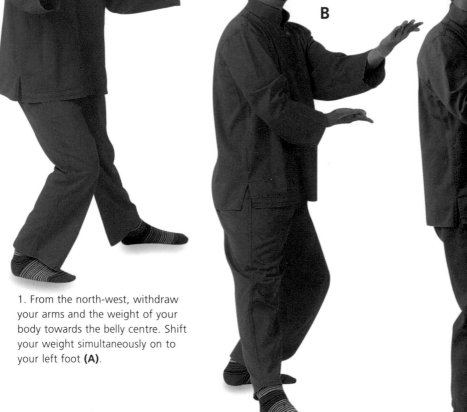

1. From the north-west, withdraw your arms and the weight of your body towards the belly centre. Shift your weight simultaneously on to your left foot **(A)**.

2. At the same time, glide the right palm under your left arm towards the elbow. Shift your weight on to your right foot, while you glide the right palm up above the left palm **(B, C)**.

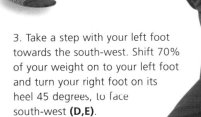

D

E

F

3. Take a step with your left foot towards the south-west. Shift 70% of your weight on to your left foot and turn your right foot on its heel 45 degrees, to face south-west **(D,E)**.

4. Moving from the torso, shift your arms up into *Fair Lady Works at Shuttles, Facing South-West* **(F)**.

POSTURE 32C

Fair Lady Works at Shuttles, Facing South-East

You return to the Lake and see every experience in your daily life as a mirror reflection of your true self.

1. From the south-west (see previous spread), withdraw your arms and the weight of your body towards the belly centre. Glide the right arm under the left arm, while you shift your weight on to your right foot. Turn your left foot inward as far as you can, towards the north. Keep most of your weight on the right foot. At the same time, bring your right palm under your left hand to make them parallel to each other **(A)**.

A

B

2. Shift all your weight on to your left foot. Pivot some weight on the front of your right foot and turn the back left foot **(B)**.

C

Take a step with your right foot towards the south-east. Shift 70% of your weight on to your right foot and turn your left foot on its heel 45 degrees, to face south-east **(C)**.

D

E

5. Moving from your torso, shift your arms up into *Fair Lady Works at Shuttles, Facing South-East* **(D, E)**.

POSTURE 32D

Grasp the Sparrow's Tail, Ward-Off, Left

In your open heart, you hear the courtships of animals and of humankind as blissful dances of Yin and Yang. You watch with compassion the search of Yang by Yin and Yin by Yang. There is a deep yearning within both principles to find creative union in the Tao.

1. From the *Fair Lady Works at Shuttles Facing South-East* pose (see p. 121), shift your weight on to your left foot, and glide your right palm under your left arm towards the elbow **(A, B)**.

2. Your right palm glides above your left arm into a ball-holding position **(C)**, in the same direction as in Posture 3 **(D, E, F, G**, see also pp. 28-29**)**. All the movements are co-ordinated from your waist.

A

B

C

D

E

F

G

3. The next step is a repetition of Posture 4 (*Grasp the Sparrow's Tail, Ward-off, Right,* see p. 30), in the same direction. This is followed by a repetition of Posture 5 (*Grasp the Sparrow's Tail, Rollback,* p. 31), in the same direction. After that, repeat Posture 6 (*Grasp the Sparrow's Tail, Press,* p. 32) and Posture 7 (*Grasp the Sparrow's Tail, Push,* p. 34).

4. The final position is the repetition of Posture 8, *Single Whip,* in the same direction (see p. 36).

A

The next step is the *Squatting Single Whip* sequence.
1. Starting from *Single Whip* **(A)**, turn your right foot on its heel to the right as you draw back and lower your body so that you are squatting over your right foot **(B, C)**.

B

C

D

2. Simultaneously, draw your left arm inward, back to your right thigh. Sink and describe a downward arc with your left hand along your left leg and forward, as you turn on your left heel 45 degrees to the left **(D)**. Your right hand is kept in a bird-beak formation. Your left hand is beside the left knee.

HOMEWORK 9

1. Go through the following sequences slowly, many times: *Turn and Strike with Heel, Brush Knee and Twist Step, Step Forward, Descend and Strike with Fist* and *Fair Lady Works at Shuttles.*

2. (Optional) What is the inner connection to the Yin, Yang and Tao principles? (If you have a copy of the first book, *15 Ways to a Happier You,* to hand, you may find page 86 useful.)

3. What, in your opinion, is the Spontaneous Chi Combustion Effect and how do you think it works?

4. In the *Fair Lady Works at Shuttles* sequence, imagine you have a thread holder in your hand and that you are weaving as in the olden days. Meditate on the spiralling motion of your arms connecting to the tan-tien.

CHAPTER TEN
Let the Universal Chi Building Society Supply You with All You Need

Our whole culture seems to be based on the principle that to have more is better. Everywhere we look, there is more on offer – television channels, consumer goods, foods, leisure activities. People all around us are demanding more pay, more benefits, more power.

THE 'SPEND, SPEND, SPEND' AND 'SPEND, CONSERVE, SPEND' LIFESTYLES

If people are fundamentally unhappy in their work, and find no meaning in doing it for its own sake, then no matter how much salary raise they get, they are sending out a 'Spend, Spend, Spend' signal; and these unhappy signals find a way of coming back multiplied in all kinds of unexpected forms. People feel unfulfilled, envious, discontented and angry, and regard themselves as belonging to that group in society who seem to be excluded from the 'Have More' majority.

Then again, there are those who try the 'Spend, Conserve, Spend' option. 'Buy now, pay later!' the advertisements scream out, with their promises of computers, cars, furniture, office equipment, etc. This is also based on the same idea that having more is better.

Because we are living in a democratic society, most people think that they have the right to choose to follow this principle if they so wish. However, it eventually leads to a dead end, and boredom, loneliness and money problems follow. It is argued that 'having more' for some people may be just what they need, although to others it may seem excessive. Perhaps there is some truth in this; but even if we accept that some people do 'need' more than others, there are, irrefutably, inevitable consequences for those who adhere to the 'have more' philosophy.

If you 'conserve more' in order to 'spend more', you create more problems. Everyone drives, works, walks and makes love. What is happening with their breath, stamina and health as they go about doing all that? Do they plan to regain their balance through meditative exercises, or do they just slump on the sofa or go to the pub for a few pints and sleep it all away? Anything external – better work and pay conditions, holidays, food, wine – may temporarily take away the stress and fatigue, but can also replace it with another kind of stress. Overworking, over-sleeping, over-eating, excessive drinking, over-exercising and over-indulgence of any kind leads to more stress in your life. The internal organs are unhappy with the 'more' culture because it inevitably brings with it more stress.

Learning how to conserve/spend/conserve your energy starts with energizing your internal organs first thing in the morning and last thing at night. And in between you learn to conserve/spend/conserve your effort. Even when you are travelling in to work. I know about stressful train journeys because I travel to London every week to teach. That is about 300 miles every week. I have my own energy-conserving exercises to practise before, during and after the journeys.

The thing that people really need to help them cope with their demanding lifestyles and find better balance with their body, is a Chi Building Society. Chi-building exercises such as Tai-Chi help them find a calmer and more relaxed way to manage their mental and emotional lives; and in the long run, there are positive 'compound interests' in store for them. It all depends how much you want to put into your inner Chi Building Society account right now.

POSTURE 34

Step Forward to Greet the Seven Stars

Co-operate and yield to the universal chi; let the seven limitless qualities of healing, unifying, pacifying, harmonizing, counselling, revitalizing and loving energy presences guide you all-ways.

A

1. From the *Squatting Single Whip* posture, bring your body up and shift weight on to the right foot and open both palms to the sky **(A)**.

B

2. As you sink your palms to the side of your abdomen, form fists with your open palms **(B)**.

C

3. Shift your weight from your right to your left leg **(C)**.

D

4. Your arms come up to make a multiplication sign with both arms in front of your chest. Your right foot is in the tiptoe position. Your right arm is outside the left arm **(D)**.

POSTURE 35
Step Back and Ride Tiger

Centre yourself to feel courageous chi coming forth from your tan-tien. Breathe deeply and strengthen your chi by conserving your energy before spending it.

1. Bring both palms down in front of your belly centre **(A)**.

2. Take your right foot to the back of your left heel 45 degrees **(B)**.

3. Shift your weight on to your right foot. Turn your left foot on your heel. Press down on your toes, and lift up your heel **(C)**.

A

B

C

4. Simultaneously, your right arm circles round from the back **(D)**.

5. Your right hand comes to the side of your right ear, and your left hand glides to the side of your left thigh **(E)**.

D

E

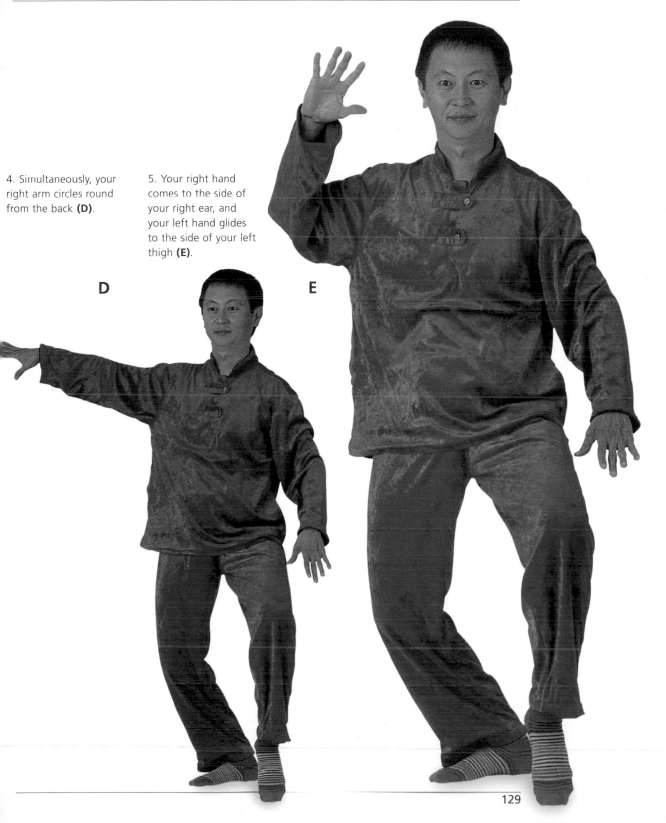

POSTURE 36
Turn Body to Sweep Lotus with Leg

Limitless, universal, radiant chi circles round you which spark off endless creative possibilities in your life to attract all that you need.

A

1. Gently sink right arm downwards in a semicircular movement towards the left side, and lift up both left and right arms to the left side **(A, B)**.

B

C

2. Take the left foot and step over to the right side of the right foot, keeping your right foot very still while you do this **(C)**.

D

E

3. Do your best to align the left heel with the right heel **(D, E)**.

F

4. Next, shift half of your weight on to the front part of your left foot and the other half on to the right heel. Balance your body in between these two pivotal points **(F)**.

G   **H**

5. Turn the body around so that you are facing west. At the same time, your right arm crosses from under your left arm to form a parallel formation with both arms (**G, H, I, J**).

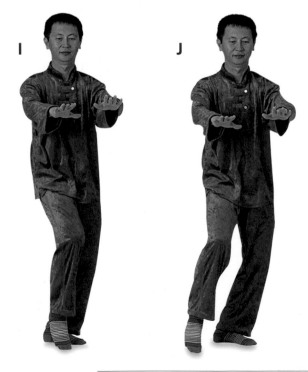

I   **J**   **K**

6. Make three small circles with your right foot and raise it to kick under your palms (**K**). The toes of your right foot make a slap-ping sound as your foot passes the centre of your palms.

POSTURE 37

Bend Bow and Shoot Tiger

A

All your goals are realized right now. You have the wisdom of Nature within you and you trust the chi energy to fulfil your destiny.

1. Following the *Lotus Sweep* posture, allow your right leg to drop down naturally in slow motion, one step forward (you are facing west). There is a square space in front of your feet **(A)**.

2. Swing in slow motion both your arms to the right side of your abdomen **(B)**.

3. From your tan-tien, swing both arms up, left fist to the front and right fist to the right ear **(C)**.

B

C

POSTURE 37B

Step Forward, Deflect Downward, Parry and Punch

1. Shift your weight on to your left foot, and raise your right foot **(A)**. Turn your waist and let your right foot and arms follow into a spiral forward movement **(B)**.

2. Repeat Posture 14 (*Step Forward, Deflect Downward, Parry and Punch*, see pp. 56-58) in the same direction. Note how the punch is formed **(C, D, E, F, G)**.

E

F

G

POSTURE 37C
Withdraw and Push

A

This is a repetition of Posture 15, *Withdraw and Push* (see pp. 60-61), in the same direction.

B

C

D

POSTURE 37D
Cross Hands

This is a repetition of Posture 16, *Cross Hands* (see pp. 62-65), in the same direction.

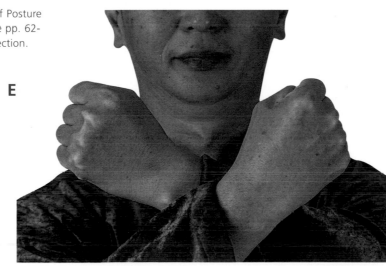

POSTURE 37E
Conclusion

*Relax, separate both your arms and slowly lower both
palms down to the sides of your thighs.*

A
(side)

A
(front)

B

HOMEWORK 10

1. Go through the following sequences: *Step Forward to Greet the Seven Stars*, *Step Back and Ride Tiger*, *Turn Body to Sweep Lotus with Leg* and *Bend Bow and Shoot Tiger*. Jot down any personal insights into the movements.

2. Do a self-portrait depicting the seven radiant qualities and colours of your self.

3. Look up some news articles and pick out a conserve/spend/conserve story; a spend/spend/spend story; and a spend/conserve/spend story.

4. List the activities that help you to conserve your chi energy, and those others that seem to drain your reserves. By changing your attitude, you may be able to do those difficult tasks you know you have to do at some point both successfully and enjoyably.

When I began learning T'ai-Chi, my first experience of chi itself was an exhilarating sense of oneness with what I can only describe as a Light Being. This happened while I was attending the school of Master Huang, a very well-known Karate Master who had given it all up to pursue his T'ai-Chi studies. He had a very down-to-earth approach suffused with a childlike light-heartedness balanced with wisdom. When I shared my experiences with him and his teachers, he would just smile. This gentle smiling light has now been shining for many years, and has helped me keep on track through all the ups and downs, curves and narrowest bends of my life. The whole T'ai-Chi Form is for me a journey in the dimension of the Light Beings. We can sometimes see them in the faces of people on the streets. Why only 'sometimes'? Because we 'see' them with our inner light, when we are sufficiently slowed down. A stranger sends you an innocent smile. You smile back. What was in that smile? A flash of light smiling in your heart, making you feel full and happy. Multiply that a billion times, and let it flood through your whole body. That is where you will find the dimension of the Light Beings.

Happiness Is Dancing with the Light Beings

The first step is the last step, the last step is the first
step in the Journey of Happiness,
The beginning and the end are always there, in the
boundless spaces of your T'ai-Chi steps.

On the plains, to the mountains, down in the
valleys, in the rivers flowing back to the seas, within the
cities, towns and villages, the T'ai-Chi Dancer awakens
with the morning's first golden rays.

Take a walk into the park and greet Nature.
Luminous violet, indigo, blue, green, yellow, orange, red,
leaves and flowers, singing silent songs to your soul.

In the golden mist, you see the squirrels, doves, swans,
ducks, crows and robins greet you,
And all around indescribable harmony, alertness and
gracefulness flow in every move they make.

Slow down, come closer to the moist ground, look, do
you see those dew drops? Be still and melt into their
tiny, fluid prisms of colour. Radiant light beings from
the sunrise greet you. They will show you the real
Rainbow T'ai-Chi and tell you we have been this way.

In your daily life, you have always loved the light in
your loved ones' eyes;
This light shines on the light out there, in the homes,
offices, shops and streets, all over the planet, from the
inside to the outside and inside again;
You see, feel, touch, hear and sense the hunger for the
light of life.

Between the Yin/seeker and Yang/results you seek
Come the Light Beings, carrying the unknown Tao of
Light and Health.
In everyday problems, the search for solutions is
really about seeking balance;
Between the opposites in every situation, you will find
the Tao of Light is really you.

Every T'ai-Chi step is a mirror of steps in your daily life.
When you are hurt, you cry out for help, for comfort
and a soothing touch,

Take the step to be the Light Being of Healing;
Forgiveness embraces you with compassion.
When you feel in disarray, you seek a leader to show
you the way,

Take the step to be the Light Being of Understanding
and Unity, gently guiding your insight.
When you are feeling uncertain and lost, you ask what
is the purpose of your life,

Take the step to be the Light Being of Freedom, Peace
and Clarity, bringing you self-confidence and direction.
When you feel insecure and sick, you yearn for a
shoulder to cry on, a home to go to,

Take the step to be the Light Being of Health, Harmony
and Prosperity, holding your heart right now.
When you are arrogant and blinded by your pride, you
long for a wise friend to show you balance,

Take the step to be the Light Being of Wisdom and
Humility, listening patiently and growing within you.
When you are lethargic and unhappy, you feel listless
and reach out for energy and hope,

Take the step to be the Light Being of Joy and Vitality,
enlivening every cell in your whole being.
When you are feeling unwanted, old and uncared for,
and you need warmth and kindness,

Take the step to be the Light Being of Love, Beauty and
Courage, tingling in your whole being.

To stay in this fourth dimension of the Light Beings
Be grateful for the chi you feel in your heart and tan-
tien,
Think of words of appreciation in Golden Light,
Feel light-hearted about yourself,
Practise T'ai-Chi with all your heart, body, mind and
spirit.
Pure pre-birth chi blending with post-natal chi naturally
flows through your whole being,
Welcoming you back to the original home,
When you first began on this Planet Earth.

The Rainbow T'ai-Chi Classics

The T'ai-Chi Classics are a set of principles passed down hundreds of years ago by T'ai-Chi Masters, to help practitioners to improve their T'ai-Chi. The following excerpts are based on these classics, but brought into a modern context. They concern basic concepts with which students need to be familiar when they come to learn the Push Hands and Partner Exercises. This fresh interpretation is the result of my thirty years' experience teaching T'ai-Chi.

In any action the whole person (heart, body, mind and spirit) is light and agile, all parts connected like pearls on a thread. The chi is respected and cultivated. It is conserved internally in the organs and not needlessly exposed.

T'ai-Chi roots the chi in the feet, it develops in the legs, is directed by the waist, and functions through the fingers. When T'ai-Chi is connected to chi healing, a person can achieve greater health and vitality. The feet, legs and waist act in unison and flow in harmony. There are no hollows, projections or breaks, so that when you are advancing or retreating you can use any negative oncoming force, inside or outside the body, to reinforce your creative/healing intentions.

T'ai-Chi is based on the practitioner's consciousness ('i') rather than any external muscular force ('li'). When you move upward to higher levels of consciousness, you do not forget to practise the activities that ground you in your daily life. When you develop the left side of your brain, you must not neglect the right side. When you advance to achieve your goals, you acknowledge that there is also a time to let go and retreat back to your heart and tan-tien centres. This applies to everyone, in day-to-day living, not just to those people whose jobs or roles in life are creative or nurturing. If you want to pull something upwards, you have to go downwards to pull it up. Likewise, to rise higher in your consciousness, you

must penetrate to lower depths to study your root belief systems and sever those that promote weeds of self-doubt and fear. With sufficient patience and time, the student can use self-destructive tendencies as catalysts for creative personal transformation.

Every part of the heart, body, mind and spirit has both a 'Full' and an 'Empty' aspect at any given time. The whole person considered as a single unit is also like this. All the components of the whole person are flowing together without interruption. T'ai-Chi Chuan is also called Chang ('long river') Chuan because it flows unceasingly, like a unending river.

Co-ordinating the Fullness and Emptiness Principle

T'ai-Chi comes from infinity; from it springs Yin and Yang. In all movements in Nature the two act independently. In stillness, they melt into one. There is no waste in the universal law of T'ai-Chi in Nature.

You yield at the slightest pressure of an opposing force, and stick to it at its slightest retreat. This principle can be applied in every area of experience – when you are 'attacked' by a pain in your body, for example. The T'ai-Chi response to the overpowering force is called the 'Tsou', or 'yielding' principle, and the T'ai-Chi initiative to improve relations with the strong force is called the 'Chan' or 'Flowing' principle. You respond quickly to fast action, slowly to slow action. Although the changes are numerous, the principle remains the same. Consistent practice develops the sensory organs of hearing, seeing, touch, smell and taste. It also increases your confidence in the power of chi to help you achieve your goals in a spontaneous and effortless way.

The chi flows from your heart to your tan-tien, down the hui-yin (the perineum – the area between the genital organs and the anus), up your spine to the top of your head and down again to your heart and tan-tien. The body remains erect but fluid, and is rooted in the feet. When the opposing force brings pressure on the left side of your body or brain, you empty that side into the Wu-Chi/Universal Emptiness Principle. The same goes for the right side. When the opposing force pushes upwards or downwards against you, it feels as if there is no end to the emptiness it encounters. When it advances against you, it feels the distance as vast (as if a person is shouting to you from the opposite end of a football field). When it retreats, it feels as if you are close to it, intimately being with it.

You are aware of the tiniest of tiny sensations on your skin because your entire body feels so light. Your body is flexible, like a reed dancing in the wind and river. The opposing force cannot detect your moves, but you can anticipate its movements. If you can master all these techniques, you become a multi-dimensional being of chi.

The Wu-Wei Principle

In Chinese, this means 'inaction' – the fusion of the Yin and the Yang principles into an effortless action. Many Martial Arts experts interpret this as an effortless punch or move that has pure emotion in it. We can see from Bruce Lee films and other Chinese kung-fu classics just how this principle can be executed with awesome precision.

In Rainbow T'ai-Chi, we are interested in how the Wu-Wei Principle mirrors what is happening inside us. There is an internal battlefield that needs to be recognized for what it is: an internal system of self-defence. Many great Martial Arts masters often say, 'You are your own worst enemy. You deal with your inner demon selves and you will win the outer battle of life.'

The Rainbow Tai-Chi Push Hands and Tai-Chi Partner Exercises sections of this book amply demonstrate the practical benefits of this principle. Its psychological and internal aspects are intrinsic to the physical practice. In one simple exercise called *Sticking Hands* (as in the Vertical Circular River Exercises) you follow someone else's hand movements. The hands are flowing with each other from the tan-tien, and when one person adopts a Yin/supportive hand position, the other person has a Yang/heavy-relaxed feeling in their hand. The Yang hand rests on the Yin hand of the other person, and then they take turns to exchange roles. The natural melting sensation of becoming Yin if you have become Yang before and vice versa produces an involuntary sensation of oneness and 'effortless effort'.

Learning How to Flow with your Aggressive Self: a Student's Experience

After practising Sticking Hands *with me, Tim sat down and we talked. He shared his wish that he could learn to flow in such a way with his wife. I suggested that they should come to do a session with me together.*

I asked Tim how he was feeling inside himself. He replied that he felt a lack of energy, restless and unwell. When he looked inside, he saw where most of his energy went. He saw many aggressive Tims. I asked him to go inside himself and practise 'sticking' with his aggressive selves, one by one. If one of them were to rebel, he should stick with him and give him infinite space to be what he wanted to be. At the same time, Tim was feeling what was happening inside. He stayed still and practised this internal 'sticking' exercise.

After about 5 minutes, he said, 'I feel at one with this aggressive self. I can feel his need for attention, for acceptance. I just stay with him as he is, flowing with whatever he feels. I feel peaceful and energized now. Wow!' I asked him to breathe in and out from this peaceful, energized feeling, and then to prepare to 'flow' with yet another aggressive sub-personality. At the end of the session, he felt bright and cheerful.

Rainbow T'ai-Chi Push Hands

Traditionally, T'ai-Chi Push Hands is considered to be part of Martial Arts. After practising and teaching T'ai-Chi for more than thirty years, however, I have discovered a deeper and more positive way to benefit from T'ai-Chi Push Hands.

Most T'ai-Chi schools only focus on the external T'ai-Chi Push Hands technique. In the Rainbow T'ai-Chi Push Hands method, the emphasis shifts towards teaching students how to do it not only with another person, but also with their own *inner selves*! The object of this is for students to learn how to harmonize the Yin/receptive and Yang/assertive principles, so that they can enjoy better health and vitality, and improve their relationships. It is a positive exercise system, which helps T'ai Chi students find more balance and self-confidence in their daily life.

I met a great T'ai-Chi Master not long ago. He had a grown-up son who was three times Chinese Champion in T'ai-Chi Push Hands. In China, T'ai-Chi Push Hands competitions can be very different from the T'ai-Chi Push Hands in the West. You are liable to suffer broken bones, damaged limbs and concussion! Despite his experience in these competitions, I witnessed the son suddenly become like a mouse when he was in his father's presence, and I could see that the father, although a famous calligrapher, poet and painter, did not know how to appreciate his son. I said to both of them, with heartfelt tears, 'Look, both my own parents are dead now. My father, too, was a Martial Arts master. One thing my father and I nearly failed to do before he died was to express our love for each other. Luckily, in the end, my dad and I were able to connect heart-to-heart before he passed away. And I don't want you two people to miss that opportunity.' I got both of them to acknowledge the situation, and suggested that the father could write a love poem dedicated to his son. After this, we all burst out laughing, and there was a lot of affection flowing all around.

In China, for thousands of years, the Confucius philosophy stopped parents from being spontaneous and affectionate with each other. Parents were not even allowed to laugh and make jokes with their children, and many parents, including T'ai-Chi Masters, still find this difficult today. So, although one may be a great T'ai-Chi Push Hands expert, the heart may not have been courageous enough to push away the blockage and neutralize it. I also showed the T'ai-Chi Master how to discover Yin in Yang and Yang in Yin in our inner Rainbow T'ai-Chi Push Hands way, which encourages loving co-operation rather than competition and rivalry.

When we look at the crises in the world – terrorism, disease, floods, famines, war and political instability – the underlying challenge facing the people trying to cope with these problems is to deal with Yin vying with Yang. The Yin group wants Yin changes while the Yang group wants Yang solutions. But in any crisis, if both factions really practise T'ai-Chi Push Hands, they will discover that each one has both Yin and Yang within them, and they will achieve a balance that enables them to flow and co-operate with each other. The emotional, mental and spiritual opposites within the world's leaders need to be harmonized first before they try to negotiate with the opposition.

In the Rainbow T'ai-Chi Push Hands exercise, we still practise with a partner, but we use the external experience as a stepping stone towards greater self-understanding and self-transformation. There are basically four principles in Push Hands: Ward Off, Roll Back, Press and Push.

Ward Off

This concept is concerned with neutralizing an opposing force. By making contact and sticking with the oncoming force, we have the chance to neutralize it. The oncoming force is naturally in an assertive, Yang state, requiring the balance of a corresponding, receptive Yin state to cancel it out. In daily life, you sometimes meet a friend who is quite angry. If you have a very receptive, listening, non-judgemental and neutral attitude towards him, he feels your presence is helpful. Conversely, if you are in an angry mood and you meet a friend who is also upset about something, both of you are in a Yang state, and will not balance each other. So, you *ward off* potential conflict by adopting a Yin state and balancing out the Yang aggression.

Rollback After neutralizing the oncoming Yang/assertive force with a Yin/receptive attitude, you can 'borrow' that force. It is like collecting little twigs for a fire and making them into a nice bundle. You roll them all together, to be ready for use. This requires a great deal of flexibility. Even rocks that fall from the hillside must roll while they fall. T'ai-Chi Push Hands can be seen to have a 'Rock and Roll' effect. You learn to roll with any hard force coming your way. When I think about this, what often comes to mind is this old-fashioned potato-washing machine I once used. I would put lots of potatoes into it, with water, and it would not only clean the potatoes but also peel off the skin, too. The potatoes rubbed against each other and the friction both cleaned and peeled them.

Press When you have neutralized the oncoming force by gently warding it off and rolling its power into your control, the next step is to hold this pressure steady. When you feel someone is depressed, they need some kind of outlet to relieve some of that pressure. That person may not feel like talking about it, but with a gentle approach, you press him to speak about it, and he will feel much better after sharing it with you in a frank manner. Remember to apply minimum pressure, which is more like a feeling of encouragement.

Push When you are dealing with conflict, pushing for a creative solution on a practical level and directing energy towards a positive result are very important at this last stage. We are concerned here with directing the transformed, opposing force back to where it came from. Now, if you have the intention of hurting this opposing person, you may direct this energy to do him injury. However, if you are intending to help him, your push towards him will give him positive energy. In a dynamic context, ideas are useless when they are not grounded in practical action.

In order to help you understand how this internal Push Hands actually works, I would like to share with you the personal accounts of some of my students. Each person's internal Rainbow T'ai-Chi Push Hands experience is unique, and the positive results are unpredictably wonderful! By learning to 'Ward off' or 'Neutralize' any negative energy (Yin principle) and 'Roll' or 'Flow' with each self in an accepting way, we discover what each self needs. Then we go on to 'Press' or 'Affirm' the kind of positive energy (Yang principle) the self requires, and to help it discover that this is actually already present, behind that negative force. The next step is to 'Push' or 'Encourage' – effortlessly – the self to become more balanced, confident and relaxed. These inner experiences of gentleness, oneness and peace are energizing, and help the person to feel more integrated and whole.

There is an ancient Martial Arts saying that states: 'You are your own worst enemy. When you win "you" over, no one can defeat you.' T'ai-Chi wisdom takes this proverb one step further: 'Make friends with your inner enemies and they are your friends for life. They will help you achieve your goals in your outer life.' What is important, however, is the application of the principle in daily life.

The Dynamic Process of Self-Knowledge:
Mark's Experience
I started practising T'ai-Chi at a T'ai-Chi School in London, about 10 years ago. The major emphasis of the Push Hands exercises was to develop Martial Arts attack and defence capabilities. We would literally spend hours and hours pushing hands with other members of the class. We were striving to yield and soften ourselves to our opponents, but there was no study or discussion about how the Push Hands principles could relate to the dynamic relationship between the different parts of ourselves. We were taught to listen for our opponent's attack, yield to our opponent's push, then neutralize his force, and return his energy back to him.
What really excites me about the Rainbow T'ai-Chi Push Hands system is the thought that the principles of Push Hands can be applied internally. First we must listen carefully to a part of ourselves that really wants to communicate with us. To do this we must open our heart centre to be receptive to this aspect of our self.

Next we need to learn how to yield, by creating a loving space inside ourselves, then to neutralize, by allowing the heart to open further, with Yang effortlessly flowing into Yin, and by returning with the Yin energy and keeping contact with it through the loving awareness of the heart. In this way, with each minute movement in the Push Hands circle, we can share the journey of discovery and healing with all those inner aspects of our selves.

Push Hands with an Abrasive Self: Thomas's Experience

I'm sitting in the airport. Fifth flight this week. I feel tired. Checking in, I am sensitive and abrasive. Someone walks in front of me and I nearly trip, another takes ages to find her passport, holding up the queue, passport control has only one man on duty with at least eighty people waiting to go through.

As I sit down finally at the pre-departure gate I stick with this Thomas. Let the Push Hands begin. He feels fed up and my chest is tight. 'Why are we here? When is this going to end? This is a waste of time! I am tired, you are off to Paris to secure a contract, why? You're starting a new job in three weeks.' I sigh and stay with him. The longer I move with this Thomas, the more I sense a loneliness behind his aggression. As always, the stronger this loneliness becomes, the more it manifests itself as a physical experience. My chest feels heavy but not tight, my shoulders are heavy, too. The loneliness feels like a vacant, heavy hole in my chest. It has an emotion. I home in on this loneliness, this hole. Inner tears well up. My inner self calms but he is very sad and lonely.

I stay with this feeling. I feel the movement in my chest continuing. It feels as if I'm able to take in more air. My breathing slows. Involuntary, deeper breaths come naturally. The sadness continues to decrease. This inner self appreciates the space he is given – a space just to be, and to be acknowledged. The more I relax, the more sensitive I become to the ripples of Yin/Yang. They start very faintly but increase in intensity. More deep breaths, more ripples.... Ripples of joy. My inner self is now relaxed. My chest feels spacious, full of radiant yellow light emanating from my heart. I feel contented.

Push Hands with a Restless Self: John's experience

I am at the computer. Loads of work to do. I start. After a few minutes, a restless self appears. Wants to distract me, jump on to other things. I sit back and allow him to come forward. He becomes lethargic. He wants attention. I see a face looking up at me, almost begging, like a young dog,

except that this is a face of a boy. Heaviness in my chest. I stay with him. He is very elusive. Restless, wanting to do anything to keep active, before diving into lethargy. The intensity increases, then sadness...a deep, deep sadness. I see the boy. He is sitting on the floor, resting his chin on his knees, hugging his legs. 'It's all right,' I comfort him. I place my arms around his shoulders but say nothing. I feel a warmth in my chest. Calmness engulfs the scene. The restless feeling is gone. Everything is peaceful. I feel tingling up my arms. The boy is sitting back, less tense. I know that he has been with me a long time and his need for love is great.

Push Hands with a Rushing Self: Sandra's Experience

It is 6.15 in the morning. I am in my car driving to the airport. I am late. The anxious self is in full flow. Thoughts are being fired into my head one after the other, at manic speed. Planning ahead, seeing the future scenes.

I follow her, but allow her space. Skin sticking. My head aches slightly and there is a tightness in my chest. She is worrying about everything. More thoughts bubbling up. I give her more space. She feels exposed, doesn't want the attention, the limelight. I see a figure rushing around, always busy. She is totally obsessed with activity. Thought must follow through; there is no choice. She wants to please. Wants to make sure there are no surprises. Control the future. She is now in full flow.

An energy rises from my belly and tightens my chest. A physical movement. The more I observe Sandra, the more love I feel for her. I comfort her, acknowledge that she has worked so hard. Done her best. I tell her that she can let go a little. I am with her. She finds this very hard. It is not her nature to let go. What if something goes wrong? If something unforeseen occurs, something is not covered? She would have failed me. I just repeat that she can let go a little. It's okay, we are together and I love her. I start to relax and feel a sense of detachment. It's as if this self is starting to detach herself from her anxiety. I see her clearly. An involuntary deep breath fills my lungs and the tightness in my chest vanishes.

So, what is the ultimate purpose of the Rainbow T'ai-Chi Push Hands exercises? To help people unite their Yin and Yang energies. Many ancient Chinese Wise Principles of Immortality are revealed in the study of T'ai-Chi Push Hands. For example, Wenshi, adept of the Chinese Classics on Immortality, said:

'When the Light of Consciousness is turned around, the
energies of heaven and earth,
Yin and Yang, all fuse into pure energy.'

In internal Rainbow T'ai-Chi Push Hands, we can see the
relevance of this ancient Chinese principle of turning the
Light of Consciousness around. In T'ai-Chi Push Hands, we
deal with the four basic principles – the Receive the Push
with the Ward-off/Neutralizing principle; the Roll Back and
Transform the Yang/assertive force into Yin energy principle;
the Listening Hands that Stick and Keep the Tension and
Pressure principle; and the Push principle, which allows you
to choose what kind of energy you want to share with your
partner or aspect of your self.

The Light of Consciousness becomes clearer when you are
consciously aware of an aggressive self – an awareness that
is usually triggered by someone out there who is threatening
you. It is the moment of conscious awareness before any
physical expression of violent reaction begins. In such a
situation in the outside world, you see a pair of angry and
glaring eyes staring at you. That glaring light gives you a
clear and unmistakable feeling in your guts and heart. It is
the same feeling you get when you are driving down a dark
stretch of road at night, and a passing car flashes its lights at
you. Danger ahead!

To practise Push Hands, you need to adhere to the following
guidelines:
1. Practise the 'Gentle Cornering of Yourself'. You agree not
to escape into other activities or emotions
.2. You must take responsibility for the way you respond to
the reactions of the selves within you. Stop talking about it,
unless your instructor asks you to do so.
3. Stop yourself projecting blame, aggression or
defensiveness. You can, with advanced practice, still conduct
a normal conversation with a person even though you may
hold an opposite point of view.
4. Learn to practise this with your T'ai-Chi heart. Heartbeat

listening is a very important part of the preparation for Push
Hands (see page 23).
5. Slow your mind down and learn to be aware of minute
movements during the moments when you are in touch
with the self within. This can feel as if you are inside every
micro-inch of the movements while you are practising Push
Hands or Sticking exercises.
6. Be non-judgemental when interacting with your inner
self (the self who is working with all the other selves is
called the 'T'ai-Chi self').

Practical Daily Application
When you are speaking with someone who is close to you,
be aware of how your inner selves are triggered. You may
find yourself suddenly feeling irritated, for example.
Although eventually you can practise internal Push Hands in
front of the person who seems to have irritated you, initially
you may need to walk away and sit down somewhere
quiet.

Watch this irritated or upset feeling welling up inside you.
Feel this part of you. Visualize it in you. It could be a restless
and lonely child inside you, looking ferociously at you and
at the person you were talking to... feel it. (You are applying
the Push Hands principle right now.)

You are flowing emotionally with this upset self, sticking
closely to it. If it is running, you run with it. If it is hiding in
a corner, you stay with it in that corner. If it wants to run
away, you stop it and corner it. This gentle art of cornering
has to be learned – it is not something that is going to
happen naturally. As you neutralize the negative feelings
through genuinely accepting this self, it may suddenly be
aware that someone is listening at last, and you may feel a
strange calmness come upon you. This is normal.

From this tranquil state, you can return to your inner self
and discover a sense of oneness and peace. And then you
may carry on describing what it is that has irritated you, in a
calm and lucid way.

T'ai-Chi

Partner Exercises

Letting Go of the Shoulders

Many people carry a lot of tension in their shoulders as a result of 'shouldering responsibilities'. This T'ai-Chi partner exercise will help you let go of all the tightness in this area. The object is to teach the body to become like a rag doll, while maintaining a connection between the belly centre and the earth.

1. Face your partner **(A)**. Push their shoulder and let your partner transfer the weight of the body on to the other foot. For example, when the right shoulder is pushed, the person goes with the flow of the push and yields,

2. Shifting the body weight on to the left foot **(B)**. The same principle applies to the other side when it is pushed: the person empties the body weight on to the right foot by turning the waist to flow with the oncoming force. In the T'ai-Chi Classics this is known as the 'Law of Substance and Non-substance'. When both people are confident of the basic moves, each should take turns to close their eyes to do the exercise. Allow the push to come without having to see it come.

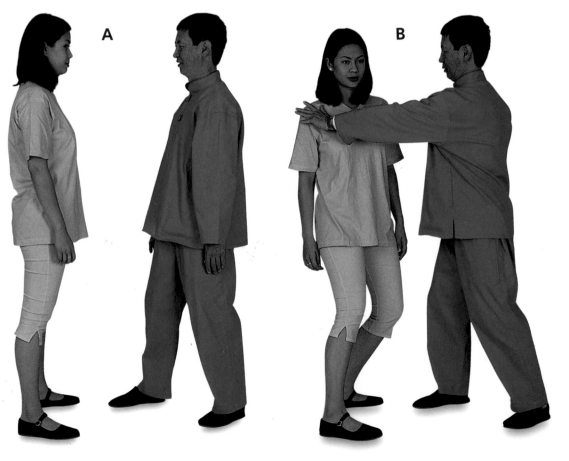

A

B

Letting Go of the Ego

After practising the above exercise regularly, you may wish to go on to do more ego-relinquishing exercises. The person who is being pushed has to have their eyes closed, as before. The challenge this time is to have fun learning to enjoy being pushed around. And of course your partner gets the chance to learn to enjoy pushing you around. Then you swap roles. Do the exercises below gently at first, and then increase the speed of the push when you and your partner feel quite confident and want more of a challenge.

A

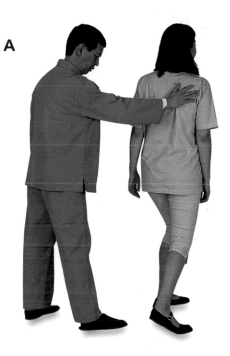

The next step is to push the thigh **(A)** and alternate it with the other thigh. The back of the shoulders is also important. When you are pushed on the right side, you shift your body weight to the left, maintaining the tan-tien centre connection **(B, C)**. Then you can also move on to the neck and head, but do so gently, as some people have very stiff necks.

B

C

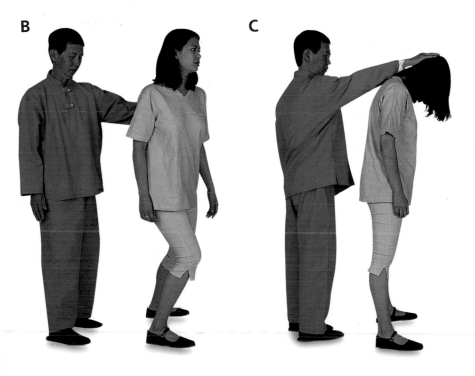

Horizontal Circular River Exercise

Imagine a river meandering through the land, passing boulders, rocks, trees, wildlife of every imaginable variety. Its movement dances round sharp corners and can be very slow and deep; it can also be very fast and dangerous.

The Principle *The art of 'horizontal communication' is about learning how to harmonize and flow with our daily outer relationships. A lot of the time the rhythms can be unpredictable and can seem extremely boring, and at other times, turbulent and cleansing, as the storms and winds push and pull everything into a swirling motion, like the spiralling Milky Way galaxy! In this exercise, you not only flow with someone but you also learn to stick to your partner.*

The four stages of T'ai-Chi Push Hands – Ward Off, Roll Back, Press and Push – are introduced at this point.

Person in red = R Person in yellow = Y
1. R's right foot is to the side of Y's right foot. R advances and pushes Y **(A, B)**.

2. Y sticks to the oncoming force and wards it to her right, neutralizing the push **(C, D, E, F)**.

3. Y presses and pushes the wrist of R **(G)**. Then it is R's turn to ward off and neutralize the oncoming force.

4. R then diverts Y's wrist gently back towards the centre, and then presses and pushes back. And the whole cycle begins again **(H, I, J)**.

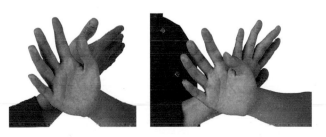

Vertical Circular River Exercise

This exercise is also like a river. As the river flows from the land into the sea, the water evaporates from the sea into the sky and falls as rain, down into the river and back to the sea again.

The Principle *Within Yin is Yang, within Yang is Yin. The potential of a person who seems initially weak (Yin) means that they can one day develop and become strong (Yang). Another way to see this is by envisaging how an overly receptive (Yin) person can find better balance and become more assertive (Yang) in his or her relationship. The speed of the movement between the two people can also change to become very slow or very fast. A most enjoyable ride! The 'very fast' rhythm is guaranteed to raise a laugh, as one person speeds up and the other person has to follow and flow with it.*

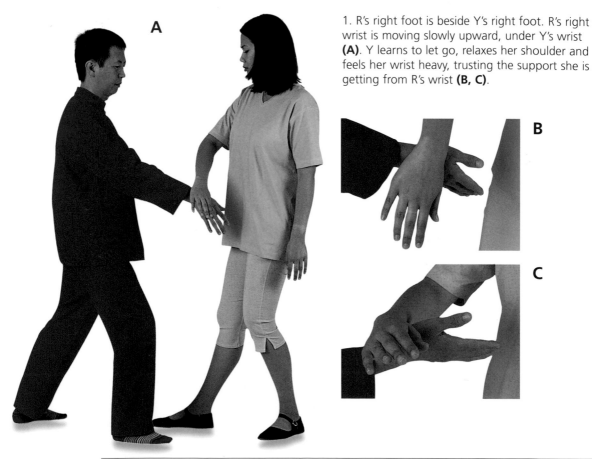

1. R's right foot is beside Y's right foot. R's right wrist is moving slowly upward, under Y's wrist (**A**). Y learns to let go, relaxes her shoulder and feels her wrist heavy, trusting the support she is getting from R's wrist (**B, C**).

D

2. As R's supportive arm goes up higher, Y's elbow raises gradually **(D, E)** and takes over the supportive role. She gradually allows the weight of her arm to let go and become heavy on R's wrist **(F, G)**. So, it is Y's turn to support R.

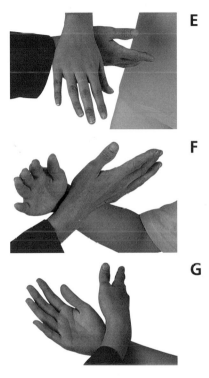

E

F

G

3. The transition is very important. R's wrist gently glides under Y's wrist **(H, I, J)** and then the whole cycle begins again.

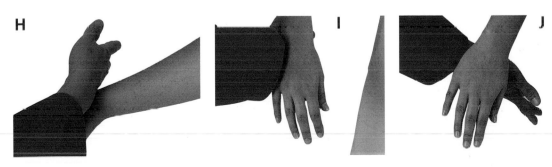

H

I

J

Horizontal and Vertical Walking Exercise

This movement is primarily a walking T'ai-Chi partner exercise aimed at bringing both partners to an even more harmonious rhythm. It also brings together the Horizontal and Vertical circular river exercises into a whole sequence. It is like swimming with a wild dolphin, up and down in unpredictable ways. Either partner can suddenly change from the one movement to the other, and the co-respondent has to flow with that change. When both people close their eyes and learn to flow with their partner on a deeper level, the exercise becomes both more exciting and more challenging, as the unpredictability factor increases dramatically .

Horizontal Circle Walking Partner Exercise

Person in blue = B Person in yellow = Y
1. Both people are doing the horizontal circle to start off. B pushes Y with the right wrist; Y wards off and neutralizes the oncoming force **(A, B)**.

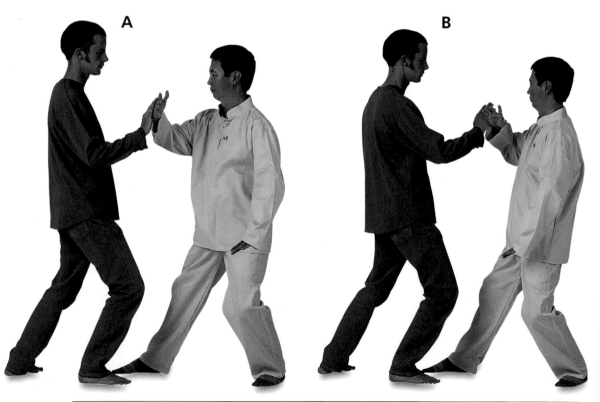

A   B

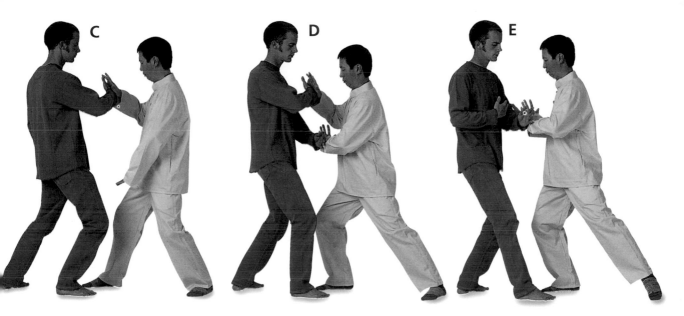

2. With right hands together, Y brings the left wrist up slowly to connect to B's left wrist **(C, D)**.

3. As the wrists connect, Y shifts his weight forward and takes a step forward with his right foot, while B takes a step backward with his left foot **(E)**.

4. The right hands are gradually released and the left wrists now connect **(F)**. They continue with the horizontal movement **(G, H)**. At any time, they can change into a vertical circle.

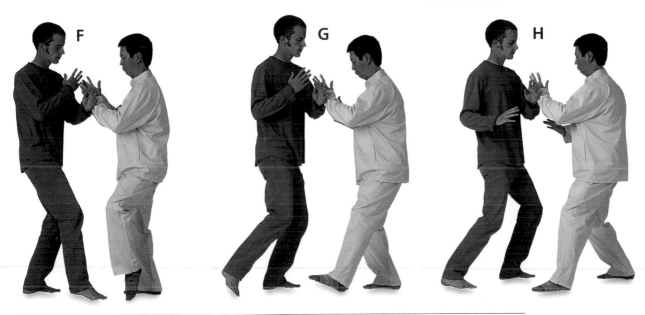

Vertical Circle Walking Partner Exercise

1. Both people start with the vertical circle.
B leans his arm on Y's wrist **(A)**.

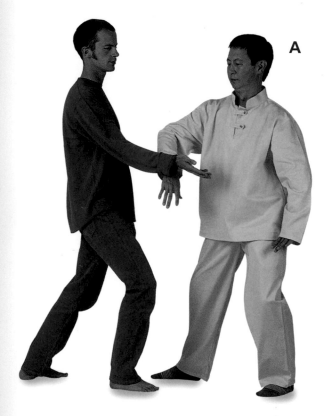

2. Gradually, Y lifts his arm up **(B)**.

3. Just before the arms drop down, Y advances, with his body weight shifting on to his right foot and bringing his left wrist to connect to B's wrist **(C, D, E)**.

4. The right hands gradually sink down **(F)** and continue with the vertical circle. At any time they can change to the horizontal circle.

157

Martial Arts Application

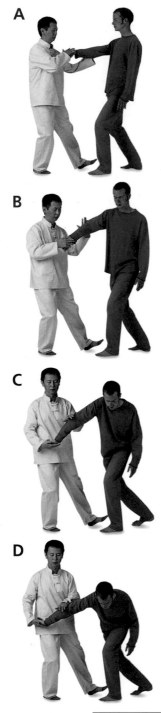

When you have reached a certain level in your T'ai-Chi Form practice, you develop an awareness of choice. You can always choose where you want to put the emphasis. So, you have 'warded off' and 'neutralized' your opponent (this could be at any level of daily life, such as a simple quarrel with a neighbour, your spouse or your office colleague). What are you going to do now? What is your intention, when you bring it up again?

You 'press' home your point. And then what? You 'push' your partner into a corner with your ideas by demonstrating how plausible they are and how thoroughly you have addressed the problem in hand.

It is from this perspective that the following exercises are shown for the first time in book format, and represent the alternative to a Martial Arts resolution. To illustrate this point fully, here are some small sequences from the Rainbow T'ai-Chi Form Posture 11b, Wheel Turning (see p. 46-7), and Posture 12, Brush Left Knee and Twist Step (see p. 48).

Person in yellow = Y Person in blue = B
1. B throws a punch at Y. Y intercepts the punch with Posture 11b, *Wheel Turning* sequence **(A)**. Y does not grab B's arm, but his palm touches B's wrist and elbow, and with a gentle twist of the waist, moves B's arm **(B, C)**. B starts to feel unbalanced and is naturally forced forward **(D)**.

2. At this point, Y has can choose whether to dislocate and hurt his arm or to stimulate the acupuncture points of B's heart meridian. If his intention is to hurt B, then, yes, he breaks his arm and causes him tremendous pain! If he wants to transform B's aggression into an opportunity to help him, then he touches his heart meridian along his arm with loving chi.

3. Continuing with the above sequence, when B is caught off-balance, he may try to escape by pulling back after being thrown towards the front. Y flows with B's intention and goes into Posture 12, *Brush Left Knee and Twist Step*.

4. At this point, Y again has a choice. Y can either send a negative force into B's chest and hurt his heart and lungs, or send loving chi into B's chest and energize his heart and lungs **(E)**.

Aqua T'ai-Chi

Introduction:

'Flowing into the Aquarian Age with Aqua T'ai-Chi'

Many people believe that we are entering an Aquarian Age, an age of loving consciousness which is expressing itself not only at community level, but also nationally, even globally. Rapid expansion in scientific, medical, technological, ecological and electronic communication networking is believed to be part of the outward manifestation of this.

In the Western world, there is an ever-increasing awareness of the need for inner development, and a rebalancing of personal communication. Western enthusiasm for alternative therapies, spiritual disciplines, environmental issues and healthy living has never been so keen.

Aqua T'ai-Chi has a significant part to play in this new movement, as it builds a bridge between the discoveries of the medical and scientific worlds and the chi energy discoveries of the heart, body and mind. Medical research has discovered, for example, that bodily organs not only contain receptor sites for neuro-chemicals of thought and emotion, but can also *create* these same chemicals. If the liver, bowels, ovaries and heart can make the same chemicals as the brain does when it thinks, we begin to see that the whole body is truly an intelligent and sensitive being in all its parts.

'Wholeness' is increasingly perceived as the natural state of well-being and the basis of good health. Aqua T'ai-Chi helps to bring about balance in the heart, body, mind and spirit. Aichi, another water-based exercise, was created in Japan from research into the Alexander Technique and T'ai-Chi principles, and shares the same focus – to help people recover inner balance and well-being. But Aqua T'ai-Chi has a more energetic and heart-centred approach to learning the exercises in water, and the exercises themselves are more detailed.

As more and more people turn to alternative therapies, techniques and philosophies to help them become healthy and confident, they naturally ask 'Why learn T'ai-Chi in water? Isn't T'ai-Chi usually learned on land?'

T'ai-Chi Chi-Kung is not an easy art to learn, especially at first. Most people say that although the benefits are wonderful, they feel tension in their bodies, especially if they have to hold their limbs in a fixed position for a long time while they are waiting for their teacher to come to them! Whether the postures are static or in continuous motion, the body's normally dormant muscles are activated.

Japanese Aichi trainer Mayumi Yano and myself at the Aichi Teachers' Training Course

When you practise T'ai-Chi Chi-Kung in the water, your muscles relax and your movements feel effortless. After this experience, I encourage people to practise on land. And they suddenly realize why for thousands of years T'ai-Chi and Chi Kung Masters keep telling students to be fluid in their movements! In the same way that water conducts electricity, your naturally fluid awareness is channelling abundant, revitalizing chi energy. It is not merely by chance that more than 70% of your body mass is made up of fluids. Nature has created a marvellous vehicle that serves as a constant reminder that you are a limitless being of beauty, vitality and gracefulness.

In all kinds of heart, body, mind and spirit healing, deep relaxation is a common ingredient for both patient and healer. A relaxed attitude, or 'effortless effort', is very important in Aqua T'ai-Chi exercises. It helps you to accelerate your healing process and increase your energy levels.

Preparation for Rinabow Aqua T'ai-Chi

If you have difficulty learning to let go and trust the water, here are a few suggestions to help you. Confidence in the water makes Aqua T'ai-Chi easier to perform.

The blindfold Wearing a blindfold can be a very important initial step before you start the Aqua T'ai-Chi movements. A blindfold helps you to relax your eyes, allows you to sink into the Wu-Chi (principle of total emptiness) and find a deep inner peace before starting your steps. An air-travel blindfold will do.

Floating The purpose of floating is to enable you to learn how to let go and trust the water. Ask a friend to support you in the water. At the Rainbow T'ai Chi school, we use float belts, which are not easy to come by elsewhere, although the principle behind them is simple. The flat piece should go on top and the round piece supports the bottom of your spine. You may need to adjust the float belt slightly to keep your whole body afloat. Tall people may need two float belts – one for the upper half and the other one for the lower half of the body. It is best to have someone helping, who can steady your direction by placing their

hand gently under your middle. When you are floating, open your arms and palms to the sides and let go completely. Become as transparent and as yielding as water. Just as water conducts electricity, your vulnerable and yielding state makes you an excellent conductor for chi energy.

Ankle weights Weights are used to anchor your body in the Aqua T'ai-Chi movements. (Some of the Aqua Tai sequences involve you sinking your whole body down and the weights keep the body under water.) Weights can be easily obtained at any sports shop.

Ear plugs If you have difficulty finding a pool that timetables a period of quiet, relaxing aquatic exercise, ear plugs may help you block out some of the activity around you and achieve a quiet mind.

Breathing

Ever since you were born, your breath has always been with you. As you grow up, you forget this and take this gift of life for granted. But it is never too late to slow down and learn. Learning how to breathe in slowly, breathe out slowly and hold your breath in a relaxed way are important steps that bring you closer to unveiling nature's secrets of health and rejuvenation. The purpose of studying the science of breathing is to enable you to discover and generate more chi.

The practice of breathing before doing T'ai-Chi in water helps you to be more receptive to the chi. This section is especially useful for people who do not feel immediately comfortable with the idea of putting their head under water. All the following exercises should be practised out of the water.

The first step is to slow your breath down and lengthen the in-breaths and out-breaths.

Many people find it difficult to have long out-breaths and long in-breaths, because they are used to hurrying their breathing. This conditioning can change with patient listening to your breath. Having longer in-breaths or out-breaths is like spending or earning money. You may think that having £100 is not very much, because you have lots of money and you are in a happy mood and feel very generous. So you spend it without thinking about the pennies that make up that £100. If you have not got lots of money and wish you had, you too may not be aware that hundreds of pounds come from pennies. If you went into a shop and had only £1 to spend, how would you spend it in such a way that you could get 10 items from that £1? You have to split it up. In the same way, when you breathe, divide one breath into ten units. With your out-breath, make a whistling shape with your lips. Breathe out in small amounts of air. When you breathe in, breathe in small, homeopathic dosages. Enjoy every little out-breath and in-breath.

1 Sit comfortably with your back straight. Align your spine to your bahui point (the centre of the top of your head). Let your in-breath come from your stomach and up to your chest, and your out-breath go from your chest down to your stomach. Follow your breathing and get to know it in a normal and natural way. Accept the rhythm of your breath – do not be tempted to judge it as shallow or incorrect.

2 Pay attention to the pauses in between your in-breath and out-breath. Naturally, the length of your in-breath and out-breath will lengthen. Being patient with your breath is important. There is no hurry.

3 Relax into the peaceful rhythms. Hold your tan-tien centre with one hand and your chest with the other. Concentrate on melting into the warm and energizing spaces of your belly and heart.

4 Tune into the Inner Child/Tao, Mother/Yin and Father/Yang aspects. With your breath of peace and loving chi, let your attention focus on the inner Yin, Yang and Tao principles, one at a time. Embrace any positive or negative feeling that wells up inside you with your breath of gentle peace.

5 Learn to enjoy holding your breath under water. If you do not like the idea of putting your head under water, the following exercise may help you. Fill a large salad bowl with water. Breathe in and hold your breath, while you try to keep your mind quiet and peaceful. Then bend your head down into the bowl. Hold your breath as long as you can, and keep extending the time. Some people manage 20 seconds, others 3 minutes. Know that at any time you can pop up your head. Progress at your own speed at this stage. You may find that you naturally increase the amount of time you hold your breath in small stages. Keep encouraging yourself.

THE BREATH OF INNOCENCE IS THE BREATH OF CHI

Feel your breathing right now.

Breathe in. Breathe out

Breathe going in, going out...naturally.

These rhythms change accordingly to accommodate the changes in your feelings. For example, pain is expressed through your breath as much as the sighs and ecstatic cries of your most pleasurable moments.

This breath has been here ever since you were born. Till now. And always will be here with you. Whenever you feel angry, hurt, happy, wonderful or sad, your breath carries these feelings into your whole body. These positive and negative emotions are recorded in your organs.

These feelings of the past have been imposed on your breath, and registered in your body.

The experiences of yesterday take away the innocence of your breath.

It is only the pure feeling of *space* that can free the breath to return to innocence.

It is like the wind that comes into your house uninvited,

You opened your window and door and there it is.

But if the air is shut in, it becomes stale and makes the room feel stuffy.

So, where can you find this ever-fresh and revitalizing wind?

Let us come back to your breath

Pay attention to the pauses in between your in-breath and out-breath.

Right now?

Yes, right now. And now, now.

Notice how the pauses seem to grow longer and longer...

The space around you feels more and more spacious.

Now, bring your hands up in front of your chest, as if you are holding a barrel...

Move it slightly back and forth again

Your palms and arms move as if they are in your lungs,

as you breathe in, let your arms float away from your body,

breathing out, let your arms come in, closer to your chest.

Feel yourself melting into this space

From innocence to innocence,

from formlessness, you may begin your T'ai-Chi.

Starting the Aqua T'ai-Chi Form

Once you have learned the Rainbow T'ai-Chi Form steps in the previous chapters, you are ready to practise in water. The experience of practising in water will reward you with a stronger sense of fluidity and chi in your movements on land.

Before you start Aqua T'ai-Chi, try to visualize yourself doing it in water. You can choose some individual sequences and practise them in water rather than attempt to do the whole Rainbow T'ai-Chi Form. The following pages will introduce you to some Aqua T'ai-Chi sequences done in solo form, as well as some partner Aqua T'ai-Chi work.

The sequences are picked from the Rainbow T'ai-Chi Form to show you how to practise under water, so if you have difficulty recalling the step-by-step instructions and principles behind them, please refer back to the earlier chapters. The poetic aspects are highlighted to bring out the philosophical meaning of the sequences and encourage the practitioner to use the movements as seed-ideas for meditation in water.

T'ai-Chi Ecstasy by the Sea.
Dedicated to the spirit of Grandfather Yong Mun Sen.

In the Golden Pool

See yourself standing in a golden yellow pool of fluid light. The water is just right, warm and gently bubbling all around you. Soft hues of radiant blue light come up from underneath you. This bluish light reminds you to relax. So you relax. Feel yourself let go. Let the warm water rock you gently to and fro. Feel your whole body letting go even more, feel yourself being embraced by this exquisite, velvety warmth. Flowing with this rocking motion, you breathe out, softly, through your mouth. And then, you breathe in through your nose. Relax into the pauses between your in-breath and out-breath. There is not a care in your mind, every thought and worry is floating away with the waves. Only silence remains. The warm water is caressing you, cradling you... melting you **(A)**.

...eel a bright orange light glowing around you. Chi energy vibrates through ...our whole body. Feel its tingling pulsate in your shoulders, elbows, knees and ankles...melting deeper, trusting the energy flow and letting go even more...deep within every cell in your body right now, energy tingling everywhere.

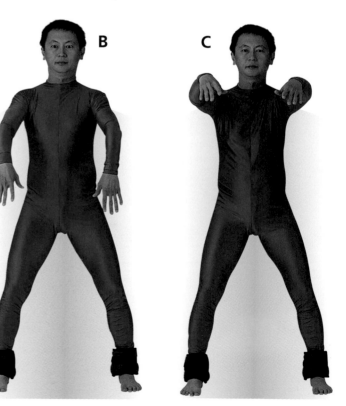

A   **B**   **C**

Slowly raise your palms up, excruciatingly slowly. With your upper arms floating up, at first you feel as if you are pushing the water. After about 4 inches of upward movement, your arms relax and allow the waves to carry you up. Right up to shoulder height **(B, C)**.

D

Let go even more as your elbows sink, allowing your arms to float and enjoy their journey down **(D)**. Feel every millimetre of the movement to be magnified. Your shoulders are sinking at the same time **(E)**; feel the space under your arms filled with tingling energy. Feel those sexy elbows loving every inch of movement; wrists follow, palms and fingers opening. Feel the electricity under your palms.

E

F

You are melting even deeper as your palms glide down to the sides of your thighs **(F)**. Welcome the First Step of the Rainbow T'ai-Chi Form. Your water journey is a fluid way home to your self. You are in the golden pool of loving chi, here right now. Every step you take in water comes from these gentle waves of chi.

The Timeless Story of Grasp the Sparrow's Tail

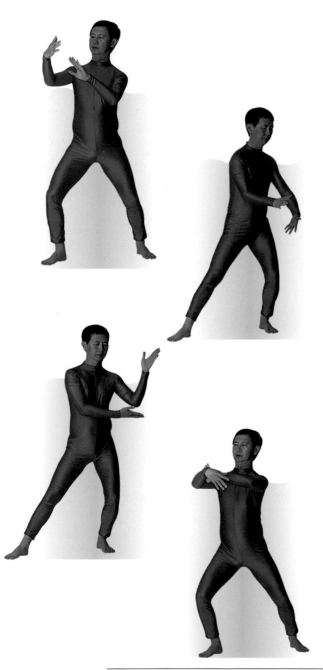

*In the beginning was Yin and Yang
Left palm is Yin, right palm is Yang
Like two fishes swimming in water
Yin running after Yang.*

*At its extreme point, Yang transforms and learns to be Yin,
the Yielding principle,
As man must learn to support woman.
The right palm comes under the left elbow.*

*Yin also discovers the Yang principle within herself
and finds quiet strength and independence.
The left palm swings to the back and takes up the superior
position; Yin and Yang fold into each other at the tan-tien,
When the left wrist and right wrist dance their way into
perfect union.*

Both gradually rising up like two fishes making love,
They glide upwards together to the highest point
and now they cannot help but part, and part they must,
As sun and moon meet for a few fleeting moments.
Both arms painstakingly fall away from each other,
micro-inch by micro-inch,
There is such delicacy when lovers part at the height
of passion.

Elbows drop down to the sides.
Every movement is suspended in timelessness.
All the space underneath the arms feels like cotton wool.
Palms sinking together in slow motion,
Turning like divers coming effortlessly to the surface,
Fingers vibrating silently with tingling chi energy.

Yin and Yang flowing in harmony,
Being with each other and yet not with each other,
Sinking into the sea of chi energy in the belly again;
To look up into the sky again and take a fresh breath
in sky-fields of golden clouds
gliding, dancing and making T'ai-Chi seem so effortless.

The Wheel Turning

Turn within.
Hear the call of your true, fluid self,
Return to who you truly are,

Life is like a water-wheel turning slowly,
Lessons you thought you had learnt keep coming back,
again and again...

You were born a being of purity in your mother's womb,
Pre-birth chi in your tan-tien surrounds you in a watery home,
Liquid food flowing to you through the umbilical cord.

Turn within,
Find the vertical circle guiding you back to the beginning
An inner world of spontaneity,
innocent smiles and chuckles bubble up from within.
All the world is seen with awe and wonder
Every self awakening to its transparent nature.

The baby born from fluid warmth becomes the child.
The child seeks the assuring warmth and smiles of the outer
parents.
Post-natal chi grows outward.

When you look upon life,
you see pulsating warmth flow through –
birthdays, graduation ceremonies, Christmases, New Year
celebrations...
Beaming faces and the encouraging voices of friends and relatives
are like
fleeting visions of light dancing on waterfalls.
Even stormy times of wanting and darkness are seen as transitory
stages along the river of life.

The older you get, the more the wheel turns around, from the periphery towards the centre.
You want to be young and full of vitality again. They tell you that you are wise, and wonderful to have around. You want to be loved, respected and given a rightful place to serve.
As a grandparent your life revolves around the young.
You wonder where the years have gone.
The search for pre-birth chi, for youth and rejuvenation, is a search for who you truly are.

The outward trappings slowly lose their hold on you.
Material rewards and relationships slowly begin to mellow down.

Turn within
to find the true chi energy you seek.
In your breathing, all selves melt into one simple place, the watery warm palace of the tan-tien awaits those who are patient.

The outward trappings slowly lose their hold on you.
Material rewards and relationships slowly begin to mellow down.

Turn within
to find the true chi energy you seek.
In your breathing, all selves melt into one simple place, the watery warm palace of the tan-tien awaits those who are patient.

The place from where you came and to where you return.
Be at home, be happy within your centre of being.

The Spiralling Power of Creative Force

*Like the sea rolling back and forth on golden sandy beaches.
Before stepping forward to achieve what you want in life,
learn to yield and allow both your arms that represent duality
to return back to the endless depth of Wu-Chi – an ocean of
emptiness.*

*In brief, surrender your
expectations that involve time. You let go of your ambition.
You have released your demands – 'I need love, I need time to
change myself, I need time to understand, I need
time to act, I need more of this and more of that in order to be
ready for the timeless dimension of creative power.'*

*You, the observer, the thinker, the perceiver and knower, are made
of time;
and when you melt into timelessness
You are free to flow into the next moment.*

*The artist, the dancer, the inventor and the meditator seek the
same goal.*

*Within the spiralling unknown of timelessness,
you find new meaning in duality.*

*Duality is embraced in the circle of timelessness, and duality loses
its power to you.*

*You are lost as another wave curves into another, and another,
until all identification ends.
Who is to judge the coming and going of universes beyond this
universe?
You are a universal being of immeasurable depth.*

*Watch as you hold the Five Elements in your right hand, and
your left palm supports your right fist to spiral forward gradually.*

You enjoy what you create, and you do not over-extend your
relationship
with the benevolent Five Elemental Presences in Nature.

As you allow your arms to fall back into endless space,
you feel yourself touching the lowest and highest crest of the
ocean of life;
you effortlessly discover the line of median.

The Law of Balance guides you into the Path of Contentment.

Single Whip and Snake Creeps Down

Before starting this movement, you need to make sure you have sufficient ankle weights for keeping your feet on the floor, especially in the last section (Snake Creeps Down), when you have to submerge your whole body.

When you feel at your lowest, very sorry for yourself,
And you seem to sink down deeper and deeper into sorrow,
Be still, hold the tension as a tree roots itself, even in stormy times.

Allow the Five Elements to support and sustain growth in apparently difficult moments.
Like a snake you spiral down silently into the water,

down, down into the bowels of the earth,

further and further until you see the planet no more,
only the void and stars all around,

alone and yet at one with the feeling.

In this emptiness, wait patiently.
The spiral of life takes you back up slowly but surely,
your spirit holds you intact; even in the saddest moments
You trust yourself and let yourself change with the situation.
Let all your negatives pass to the trees.

The water of life will always bring you up again and re-energize every cell in your whole being.
Heavenly chi, human chi and earth chi unite in you.

The Letting Go Kick

'Letting go' can be such a powerful feeling in your life,
Like ten thousand horses pounding their hooves as they gallop across the earth,
giant waterfalls thunder their way into valleys.
Shouts of jubilance fly into the air as rushing water bounces off the surfaces.

You spent your whole life enriching yourself with innumerable experiences in search of happiness.
Now is the time to release it with one burst of creative joy
And now is the time... and now is another fresh opportunity;
Every moment is a movement of excitement inside your body.
Billions of new cells burst forth and swim their way into life!

Rejoice and let Yin, Yang and Tao within come together in a lightning flash of creative insight!

Opening Windows

When you sink into your tan-tien from the Single Whip *sequence,
like water swirling into a spiralling centre,
your outstretched palms glide back towards the tan-tien,*

*Arms revolving around your waist,
The space supporting the descending
arms with such exquisite sensitivity, every
hair on your body shivers as chi dances
towards the centre of your being.*

*In the core, water and fire merge into kan and li,
they gather the dual force
into creative steam
spiralling into the heavens;
feel the earth, moon and planets in this galaxy spiral
around the sun.*

*Let the energy around you be
warm and yet so soft...its
softness shines
as moonlight reflecting in
billions of tiny shining stars.*

*Everywhere you are, in all four corners of the earth, you are
being held by lightness.
Behold the gently glowing fire of your heart unlit by the
human mind,
Receive the regenerating power of the fluid warmth rising
up from the union of Yin and Yang in the tan-tien.*

Water and fire teach the Art of Surrender.
It is not humiliation that is required of your arms when you surrender.
You cannot 'try' to flow on the periphery when you surrender.
Your shoulders need to let go.

You are being loved by the beloved chi energy presence,
every cell in your skin and every particle on the planets is held in this universal chi energy.
Head in the sky, feet in the earth.

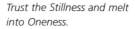

Trust the Stillness and melt into Oneness.

Aqua T'ai-Chi

Partner Exercises in Water

Holding the Chi Ball

The purpose of this exercise is to increase your chi energy supply. You can do this either by facing each other or by standing side by side. This is also a wonderful exercise to do on land. Both palms are in front of the waist. Shape your arms as if you are hugging a tree and bring it back slowly towards the tan-tien. The middle finger points slightly inward, connecting to the belly centre. Allow the water to carry your arms. You can also move the imaginary ball around in all directions, slowly and gently from the movement of your waist.

T'ai-Chi Walking

The purpose of this exercise is to increase your receptivity to chi energy through the relationship between your feet and the water and earth elements. It can be done in water as well as on land. The important aspect is to feel the space before the foot touches the floor. You can do this with one of you blindfolded, while the other holds their arm.

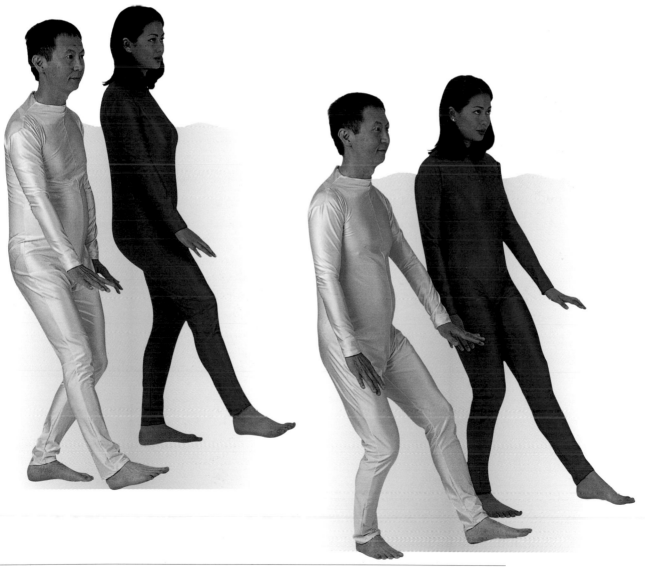

Diagonal Flying

This exercise is excellent for learning how to balance Yin and Yang communication, and although it can be done in water as well as on land, it has a very different effect when you do it on land. The sensitivity of the exercises changes dramatically. The 'heaviness' of the supportive (Yin) principle is emphasized on land, but in water the 'lightness' of learning to flow with one another in water is the important element.

A

*Both partners face each other. The right foot of one partner steps out with the left foot of the other partner towards the side. The left palm is on her right palm (**A**). Her right palm is Yin because she is supporting his palm, and his left palm is expressing the Yang principle. His right palm is Yin and her left palm is Yang.*

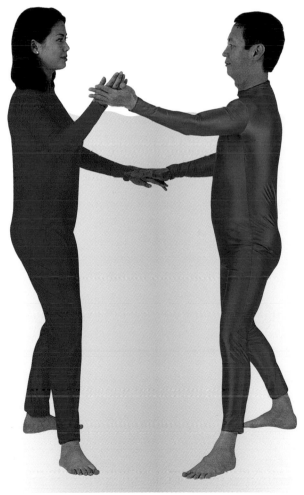

B

And then, slowly, they take a step in the opposite direction and change the position of their palms **(B)**. *His right palm is now on her left palm* **(C)**, *and her right palm is supported by his left palm* **(D)**.

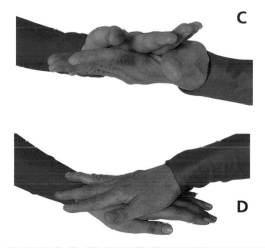

C

D

Step Back and Play with Monkey

This exercise is also about learning how to keep in rhythmic time with one another as you step back or step forward. As in a dance, you co-ordinate your movements with your partner's. When they step back, you step forward; when you step back, they step forward. Eye contact also helps to sustain the harmony in your interaction.

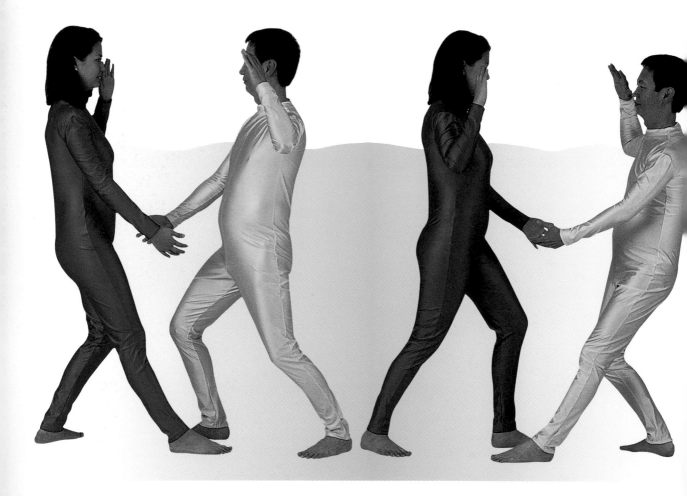

Golden Cock Standing on One Leg

This exercise is very beneficial for committed, loving couples who want to learn the Taoist way of sexual circulation. The creative sexual energy flows up the spine and down the front mid-line section of the body. This is the micro-cosmic (or small) circulation of chi. The arms take turns to rise up in co-ordination with the legs. Your partner complements you and times his/her movement to coincide with yours.

River Flowing Dance with Two Hands

*The person in blue has his hands inside, and the person in red has her hands on the outside **(A)**. She pushes forward. He withdraws **(B)** and gently twists his wrists under hers **(C, D)**. Then he is ready to move forward and she does the same withdrawal movement as he did before **(E)**.*

A

B

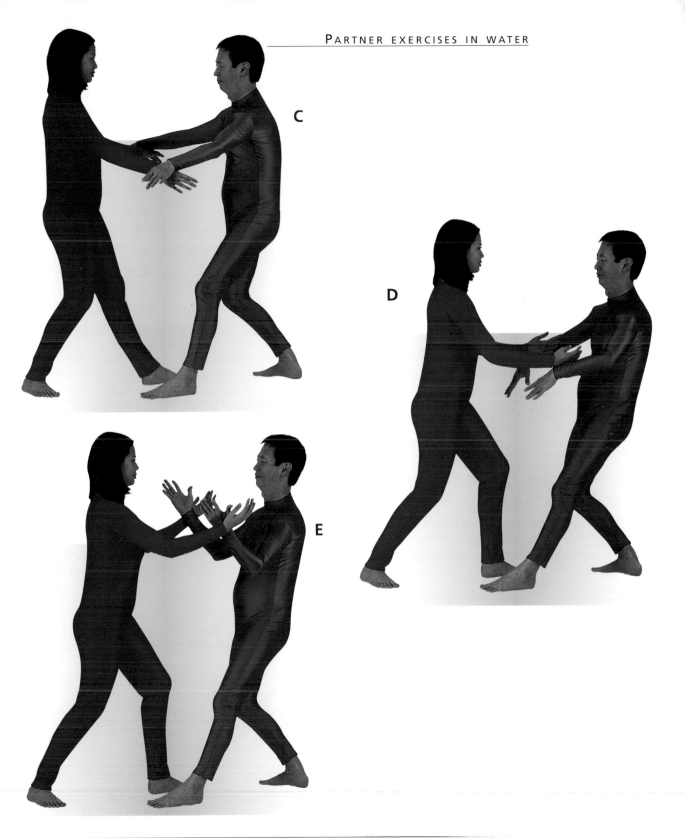

C

D

E

Couple Sunburst Kick

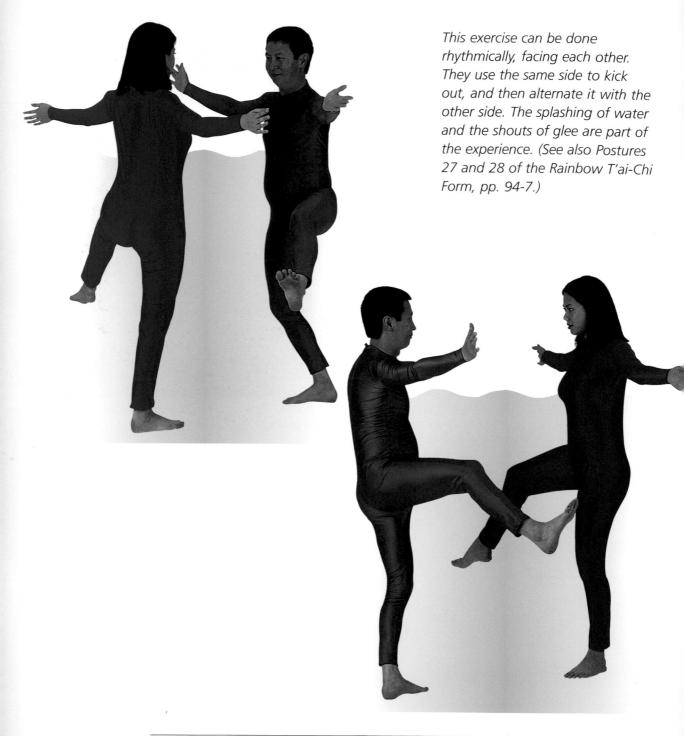

This exercise can be done rhythmically, facing each other. They use the same side to kick out, and then alternate it with the other side. The splashing of water and the shouts of glee are part of the experience. (See also Postures 27 and 28 of the Rainbow T'ai-Chi Form, pp. 94-7.)

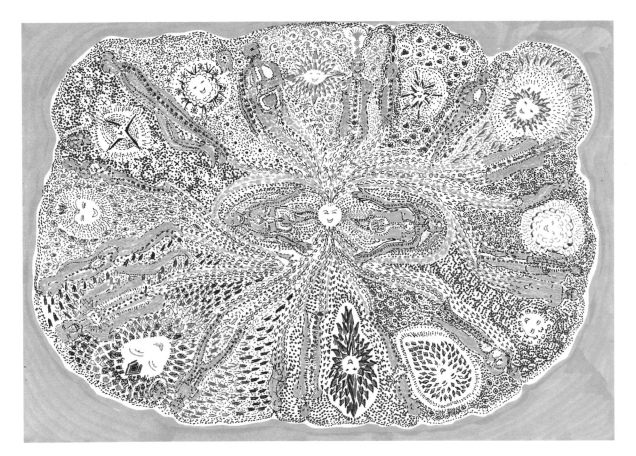

T'ai Chi Dance of the twelve primary acupuncture meridian paths of chi energy.

THE FULL STOP

(dedicated to you the reader)

A dot could be the force of an atom bomb or a thought of good.

What happens when there is a natural end to what is here?

The full stop. The full stop before the beginning of another new word.

Notice in a normal conversation,

when the 'mmmm,' and 'ahh' and the 'arhmm' comes in

to try to fill up the spaces in between the lines.

The mind grapples with what it wants to say.

And when the finishing point comes,

there may be a sigh, a cry or a smile or ache echoing inside

nothing left to hold on to, just emptiness greeting you.

Let go. Let's go into this beautiful, unknown quiet pause...

This the Chinese call *Wu-Chi*, the Universal Black Hole

inside you and outside you too. The Tao follows the *Wu-Chi* into fulfilment.

What is fulfilment? It is to be 'full of feeling for this moment'.

Let the starting point in your life be in the last thing you said.

Every step can mean a creative step when you truly let it go.

let the fullness of a long pause come into you right now.

When Nature takes its course, nurturing unfolds from within.

Just as you turn these last pages,

another chapter of your life and my life is going by...

the moment begins anew for you and me.

In between my heart-beats I pass this book into your hands,

please hold it with patience and slowly go through the difficult bits,

now and then you may forget where you put it.

Soon, it will spring up with another fresh new meaning.

Thank you for being part of my journey,

by reading these words, we have inevitably touched each other.

I hope you will join me now,

in greeting this wonderful life with yet another full stop.

Courses for Beginners and Advanced Students

WEEKLY CLASSES ON 15 FUNDAMENTAL RAINBOW T'AI-CHI CHI KUNG EXERCISES AND RAINBOW T'AI-CHI FORM

The basic T'ai-Chi Fundamental and Chi Kung Exercises and Principles build the basic ingredients of fluidity, receptivity and rootedness into your practise, while the T'ai-Chi Form is a Dance of Balance between Yin/Feminine and Yang/Masculine aspects of the self. This creative synthesis allows the practitioner to tap into a limitless, rejuvenating chi energy. As more teachers are being trained in the basic 15 Fundamental Rainbow T'ai-Chi Chi Kung and Rainbow T'ai-Chi Form techniques, more weekly classes will soon be available in many parts of the world. For a list of teachers, please write in for a copy of the current newsletter.

INTRODUCTORY WEEKEND WORKSHOPS ON THE TAO OF HEALTH AND REJUVENATION

These special weekends are held in different parts of the world. Many topics are covered, including 'Understanding the Yin/Yang Nature of Loving Chi' and 'The Art of Generating Happy Chi, How to Conserve, Recycle and Channel Chi for improving your health and vital force'. For an up-to-date schedule of these weekends, please see the quarterly newsletter.

NEW YEAR COURSE, OPEN TO ALL

There is an annual New Year Workshop at the Rainbow T'ai-Chi School where beginners as well as advanced students return to celebrate the incoming of the new planetary chi energies. It includes Swimming Dragon Chi Kung, T'ai-Chi Chi Kung and outdoor Yin/Yang/Tao co-operative games.

EASTER COURSE, OPEN TO ALL

This workshop is also held every year to encourage the rebirth of hope, self-healing and joy. The programme includes chi self-healing exercises, an Introduction to the Fusion of the Five Elements, and 'Play and Dance in a Creative Pursuit of the Tao in Nature'.

SUMMER SCHOOL COURSES

We hold two 10-day programmes focusing on the 'Tao of Health and Rejuvenation', providing a good introduction for students interested in becoming instructors of Rainbow T'ai-Chi Chi Kung and the T'ai-Chi Form.

THE FOUNDATION T'AI-CHI TEACHER TRAINING COURSES

There are two teacher-training programmes held over a period of two years. While some people do this course because they want to teach T'ai-Chi, others do it purely for personal development purposes. The first course is based on my first book, *T'ai-Chi Chi Kung – 15 Ways to a Happier You*, and the second course is based on this book.

For further details about these courses, please telephone or write to PETER CHIN KEAN CHOY, at the Rainbow T'ai-Chi Chi Kung School, Creek Farm, Woodland, DEVON TQ13 7JY, Tel: 0385 706 965/01364 653 618

Index